A GENTLE BREEZE

By Shaun Ellis

CONTENTS

PART 1 - MY STORY SO FAR

PART 2 - SELF-HELP/ADVICE

PART 3 – STIGMAS - THE BENEFIT SYSTEM - QUESTIONS & ANSWERS

Questions & Answers

1/ Can a depressed person be successful in life?

2/ Is suicide a selfish act?

3/ How can I overcome my nervousness

4/ How did you discover you were depressed?

5/ What should you do if you are depressed?

6/ Should you mix with others who have similar mental health illnesses?

7/ How can I convince my girlfriend to get help for her depression?

8/ Why do people with depression push others away?

9/ What can I do if I have a panic attack and completely freeze?

10/ What should I do if I hate my life, is a depressed life worth living?

11/ How do you recover from big failure and embarrassment?

12/ Why are some people blessed to have blissfully happy lives whilst others live in pain and unhappiness?

13/ Do people ever truly recover from depression?

14/ Do you have faith in humanity?

15/ How do you deal with depression without help from friends or medication?

PREFACE

One in four of us will suffer from a mental health illness at some stage of our lives. I am one of those people. My best friend recently suggested I should write a book about my experiences, both past and present. How I cope, and often continue to struggle with living with anxiety and depression. A depression that at its worst has nearly killed me, as it led to two suicide attempts. Like all great ideas, this conversation took place in the back room of a pub, after one too many! But nevertheless, I felt compelled to give it a go.

In the past I've had a blog, and I continue to answer mental health related questions. I like to think of myself as an advocate in getting more people to share their stories. That being said, writing this book has proved to be my biggest challenge to date.

Now, I don't profess to know the first thing about writing a book, and I apologise for the simplicity of my words. Why then am I bothering, you might ask. The truth is, I'm not sure! Maybe I need something to occupy my mind, a new project, a reason to stick around for a while longer. Maybe it will help me strive to find some answers, more understanding of why I am like I am. If anyone reading my story can relate to me, maybe I can offer them comfort of some kind, reassure them that they're not suffering alone and that their emotions are far from abnormal.

One thing I can assure you is that I'll be honest and speak from the heart. This will involve me visiting some uncomfortable places and it may be equally uncomfortable for you to read. I can only apologise if this is the case and I promise I'll try to balance the doom and gloom with some more light-hearted material.

It wasn't until 2015 that I was finally diagnosed as having clinical depression and generalised anxiety disorder. Although the truth is, I'd been battling against it much longer than this. It just took me time to find the courage to speak to my doctor. I believe my major issues (of which there's many!) go right back to high school, so that's where I'll start my story.

The names in this book have been changed to respect their privacy.

PART ONE
MY STORY SO FAR

High School Trauma

 The first thing that struck me was how tiny I was compared to everyone else. Over two thousand students in a building that was so big, I literally felt like I'd been swallowed up. As well as being overwhelmed by the enormity of it all, I also felt lost and alone, and as I wandered round aimlessly with a little map in my hand, not daring to ask anyone for directions, the only hope I had was to make some friends and to do this quickly

I'd be much less vulnerable in a group, safety in numbers and all that! I tried desperately hard to fit in, but I was far too nervous, and it seemed like everybody had already grouped off together. Panic began to set in!

My best plan now, was to try and blend in, and attempt to make myself invisible to the world. Would it be possible to accomplish this feat for five years? Sadly, the answer to that was a resounding no.

Right from the beginning I was easy prey for the bullies. Being weak, fragile, and highly sensitive is not a good combination. I was much smaller than the other kids and being on my own, I stood out like a sore thumb. My tactic of staying quiet and keeping a low profile was quick to backfire on me. I soon got the nickname of Steve Davis which I hated! But it was to stick with me for the rest of school. If you don't know, Steve Davis was a snooker player who was well known for being extremely dull and boring.

I was given several other derogatory names, such as Mr. Puny verse and my personal favorite FA cup ears! And so, began an excruciating time for me, where every day was like a living hell!

It's hard to believe just how cruel and vindictive kids can be, unless you've experienced it first-hand like me. The name-calling and intimidation were relentless, and I had to endure periods of physical abuse as well. I was thrown down an embankment into some tennis court netting, resulting in a broken nose. I was frequently used as a human punch bag. I had my dinner money stolen and, once I had stopped having the school meals, I regularly had my pack lunch tipped on the floor in front of me. I was then forced to eat it from the floor, along with any other dirt or rubbish they could find. I was cello taped to my chair and stabbed repeatedly with a compass. This resulted in my mother making an appearance, which achieved very little, making me look even weaker. If anything, it caused the treatment to get worse.

I've chosen to block out a lot of my time at high school as it's still very painful, but one more day stuck in my memory, as it involved what I view as the worst kind of bullying, - humiliation. I'd adopted my usual position, sat alone in the corner of the playground, counting down the minutes until the end of break time, whilst desperately trying to keep out of sight of the bullies. Unfortunately, today was not to be my lucky day, I was spotted and forced into the middle by a lad who although the same age as me, had a much bigger physique. This guy really loved himself, and he'd already been showing off, tensing his muscles in front of a large group of female admirers, having them feel his biceps, before he rolled my sleeve up and made me tense my arm in front of them. Then he proceeded to completely ridicule me, he had all the girls giggling and I was left feeling extremely small! Not content with this, later that day in the classroom he challenged me to an arm wrestle. I refused of course, but a few of his mates told me if I didn't, they'd be waiting for me outside the school gates. In other words, I'd get my head kicked in. Doing what he wanted seemed like the lesser of two evils. Everyone gathered around to witness my humiliation, he let me use both my hands to give me a sporting chance. But of course, he still beat me! Next came the inevitable laughter and name calling. This time I couldn't stop my eyes filling with tears. I was finally saved by the arrival of the teacher.

After that day I became extremely self-conscious about my body. I started believing that the only solution, and the only way I'd get any respect from anyone, was to get bigger. I soon became obsessed with this, and from then on, every birthday or Christmas present I asked for was related to building my body up. All my spending money went towards exercise equipment, from Dumbbells to Bull workers, leg weights, ab- pumps to pull up bars. I even got myself a toning belt, which resulted in me burning my belly! I bought myself books on bodybuilding and was constantly looking up new exercise regimes.

This obsession continued throughout high school and into my working life, things didn't get much better. If I were starting work at 8 o'clock, I would get up at 5.30 so that I could do an hour and a half workout with my Dumbbells before setting off. On arrival I would go straight to the staff room and examine myself in the full-length mirror. Not satisfied with how my arms were looking, I'd quickly get down on my hands and knees and do some push-ups before everyone else arrived.

Even to this day, I prefer winter to summer so I can remain covered up and even to this day, if I see a group of women laughing in a corner, I presume they're laughing at me.

It's perfectly normal to see all your flaws, especially when you're studying yourself so intently. Even the most beautiful people will still find things they're not happy with, if they look hard enough. We're all our own worse critics after all.

How easy is it to stand in front of a full-length mirror working your way from head to toe, highlighting all the things you're not happy with? Tiny blemishes can soon get magnified into hideous deformities. Of course, these are only visible to you and not to others around you. In fact, some of the time, what you view as an imperfection, someone else might find see as an attractive feature.

Much has happened in my life since high school (some of which I'll share with you in the remainder of this book). For years I have had to battle with my mental health, the hardest part for me, being the unpredictable nature of it. Sometimes just as you think you're doing ok and moving in the right direction; something happens that completely floors you. It's like being in a giant wind tunnel which never lets you get to your destination. You can feel it pulling you back, you can almost reach out and touch where you need to be, but when the pressure turns up a notch your sent hurtling backwards, arms and legs sprawling in the most undignified way, until you find yourself right back where you started! It's hard. It's extremely frustrating! But I've learnt to make the most of my good days and not put too much emphasis on the bad ones. Bottling up childhood emotions and somehow convincing myself that the treatment I got at school was normal, has almost certainly contributed to my illness, regular counselling sessions helped me see this.

I have anxiety and depression, but I refuse to let it define me, there's much more to me than that.

BEATING THE BULLIES!

Before I continue with the rest of my story, I thought I'd finish by offering some hope to those battling with their own hardships at high school. So, what's the answer? I wish there were a simple way of beating the bullies. I hate the thought of kids suffering the same kind of daily harassment that I did, its arguably even worse now with the introduction of social media, the horrible treatment can be even more relentless. If you're a little different, school can be tough, but after your school time is up, being unique is celebrated and will get you much further in life. I'm also aware that bullying doesn't always stop at school and can continue into adulthood.

You need to find someone (an adult) to talk to. maybe you have a school counsellor or even a favorite teacher that you can open up to. It's very hard, I know, but the treatment you're getting is not fair, so please don't put up with it. Remember, bullies are very insecure people, if there calling you names, it's probably just to draw attention away from themselves.

A great idea is to have a good outlet. At the start of my second year, I came up with the idea of a lunch timetable tennis club. With the help of my head teacher and some extra fundraising, we were able to buy all the equipment we required, and my idea became a reality. Table tennis was my savior. Suddenly I had a safe place to go every day, where a teacher was always present to overlook proceedings. suddenly, lack of friends was not an issue, I was making more than I knew what to do with!

I'm not saying you need to come up with anything as drastic as that, but sometimes when you've tried everything else, thinking outside of the box is the only way to go. maybe there are existing lunchtime groups you can get involved with, finding people with similar interests to you. Anything to stop you becoming isolated and an easier target. One thing I haven't suggested is standing up to the bully. In my case there were too many for this to be an option, but if there's one main culprit then standing up to him or her might work.

It's important not to be a victim for the rest of your life. I've already shared how body image remains a problem for me. As well as this I do have a nasty habit of planning conversations with friends in a desperate attempt not to seem boring. when you've been called dull and boring every single day throughout school, sadly you start to believe it! It's true, certain events from your childhood are bound to have a profound effect on you, but they can also make you stronger.

I have continued to play table tennis and achieved a great deal through the sport, including playing for my county. Every time I have success, I feel like I'm getting one over on the bullies. The same people who tried to convince me, that I was useless and would amount to nothing.

I've spent most of my life attempting to fit in with certain groups of people. You could say I've failed miserably at this, or you could say that it's took me until now to realize that it's perfectly ok to be different, in fact it's great! If everyone were the same the world would be an exceedingly dull place. Sometimes the best thing you can do is accept that you're unique and stop trying so hard to be something you're not. This is a brave thing to do, and people will envy you for it, they might even wish they were more like you themselves.

RESPITE

Towards the end of my time as a pupil, I saw a career advisor, to discuss my options moving forward. As you might imagine, I was extremely relieved to be leaving, to finally escape my living hell. However, I was also daunted by the prospect of entering the so-called real world! What if it was no better? What if high school turned out to be a walk in the park in comparison? My new life might be filled with even more bullies!

Although far from certain of my career choices, I decided care work might be for me. I ended up getting a placement in a day centre caring for adults with learning disabilities, this involved me working four days a week learning on the job and spending one day at college obtaining my necessary qualifications. Starting a new job is a nervous time for anyone, but high school had left me extremely fragile and destroyed any confidence I may have once had. I'd allowed others to convince me that I was useless and bound to fail. Thankfully, these fears turned out to be unfounded. The staff were all extremely kind and right from the start I felt well looked after, by a workforce that was predominately female. It felt like I was getting the giant hug I desperately craved. The younger staff seemed fascinated by me, as at the time, it was unusual for a young man to come into this sector. The older staff picked up on my timidity, as their maternal instinct kicked in. College was a similar scenario, where I was heavily in the minority, 17 to 1 to be precise! This proved much less awkward than I anticipated. The girls all took pity on me, and so, made a big effort to be friendly. I really wasn't used to this; I'd just spent five years experiencing the exact opposite. And here I was instantly making friends, each of them taking it in turns to take me out for lunch!

Unlike at school, I was able to fit into my new role very quickly. It turned out I was good at the job as well, which, of course was a huge bonus. Although still very shy and still having the same body image issues (as I alluded to in the previous chapter), this was an ideal place for me to grow. It took me a considerable time to accept that I was well liked. you see, after enduring years of being a victim, this was an unfamiliar concept to me, a big part of me expected that it was far too good to be true. Putting all my issues aside, these next few years were probably the happiest of my life. I had my first serious relationship, followed by two further long-term ones, all of which being girls, I'd met through work. Not that these relationships weren't without there complications. I wouldn't necessarily recommend dating one of your colleagues! However, awkwardness aside, I didn't regret any of them. How could I, when they helped me realise, I wasn't the complete waste of space I thought I was. On the contrary, It turned out I was desirable to some people!

Away from work I enjoyed several lads' holidays, including an unforgettable trip to Jamaica, memories of which I'll share later in the book. After years of deliberation, I finally found the courage to leave home. I lived in my bachelor pad for three years. My newfound independence was fantastic, but again, not without its complications. like most young people, I'd completely underestimated the price of living. At first, I ended up having to survive on a shoestring budget. I could easily make a block of cheese and packet of crackers last me the week! I went as far as using the work toilet more often, to save on toilet paper! I got myself a companion, a rescue cat called pepper, who I spent more money on than myself. Named Pepper for her fiery temperament, which was a complete joke, as she was the most placid, loving cat you could wish to meet, if I'd ever had an intruder in the house, I'm certain she'd have licked them to death!

Aside from being skint all the time, having my own place was great fun and exactly what I needed. The staff at work donated most of my furniture, more evidence of how liked I had become. Even the kitchen staff played their part, sneaking me Tupperware boxes full of food at the end of my shifts. They claimed it was only going to waste, but I knew the big risk they were taking, and I'll be eternally grateful for their kindness.

After my teenage years being so traumatic it's hard to believe I would ever contemplate leaving a job due to it becoming too comfortable, but that's exactly what I did. After 13 years, my day-to-day role was far too predictable, and I felt I had more to offer elsewhere. Hindsight is a wonderful thing and I often wonder what might have been if I'd stayed. Would I still have got clinical depression? Would I still have the same levels of anxiety? Anxiety that at its worst prevents me from leaving the house and has led to so many horrendous panic attacks. Would I have visited that dark place that led to me twice attempting to take my life? It's hard not to consider your past decisions but these kinds of questions can drive you mad, so I try not to torment myself with them.

I've had several jobs since my first, but none have come close to the unique family atmosphere I experienced there.

My next job was working for a mental health charity, organising drop-in sessions for adults with mental health conditions, such as depression and anxiety, symptoms which ironically, are just like what I suffer from now. It wasn't an easy job. It could be very heavy going at times. Having a room full of depressed people, the conversation often ranged from how shit life was - to the best way to commit suicide! It was my job to try and come up with ways to distract them from these kinds of thoughts and create a safe and more hopeful environment. Being around so much negativity can be exhausting to say the least, although, I can now appreciate much more about this, than I could back then. I often went home feeling mentally fatigued and completely down in the dumps. But I now realise that clinical depression is worlds apart from being down in the dumps.

6 months into the job, tragedy struck my family, as my dad passed away. I'd like to take a small break from my story to tell you a bit about how much he meant to his family and to me. I could easily write an entire book on him. How he was an amazing dad, a great friend and a huge inspiration to me, maybe one day I will. But for now, I'm going to try and sum it up in the next chapter.

A FATHER'S LOVE

On June 10th, 2010, my dad died in hospital. Over ten years have passed now, but it still feels like yesterday, and I can honestly say I still think about him every day. The shock and devastation hit the whole family extremely hard. I had to deal with many fluctuating emotions at this time, but the uppermost was complete disbelief.

I kept expecting to wake up from a bad dream and see him sat there in his favorite rocking chair, probably with a sarcastic comment about how long I'd spent in bed! It hurt me that I hadn't had the chance to say goodbye and I was angry with God for robbing me of this opportunity. I also felt an unbelievable sense of guilt that I hadn't told him how much I loved him.

I guess that's the cruelty of life, it all happened so quickly. He was taken into hospital with a suspected stomach infection and sadly never came out again.

I always viewed him as such a strong person, growing up I'd look up to him and thought of him as invincible. For a long time after his death, all I had etched on my mind was a picture of him led in the intensive care unit with countless wires and tubes hooking him up to a machine. That was the only time

I'd seen him looking so fragile, and it wasn't the way I wanted to remember him.

I never cried for my dad, not at his funeral and not anytime afterwards. At the funeral people who barely knew him were sobbing their eyes out. I remember thinking there must be something seriously wrong with me. Was I an emotional cripple, not to have shed a single tear on this day, of all days?

This lack of reaction seemed strange, but at least allowed me to continue to function properly and make sense of things. Inevitably, I took on the role of chief organiser, looking after the family finances and any correspondence that needed dealing with. At least this way, I felt I was being in some way useful.

I was happy to be the strong one for as long as my family needed me to be. I believed I would grieve in my own time. The sad truth is, I've never properly grieved for my dad. I'm desperate too, but don't know how. I hope people realise; this doesn't mean I loved him any less. I miss him terribly every day and still feel a large emptiness, which will never be filled.

One thing that helps immensely is that I'm able to wear his necklace. Every morning when I put it on, I say, 'Good morning dad' and tell him what we've got planned for the day. Every night when I take it off, I tell him I love him (Something I couldn't do when he was alive). I take great comfort in knowing wherever I go, he goes too, and I'll always wear his chain with pride.

My dad grew up as an only child in a strict family. I don't know much about this stage of his life, as he didn't like to talk about it, even with my mother. What I do know, is he was treated harshly and unfairly disciplined, throughout what was to be a very tough childhood. He was rarely praised and constantly put down, a lousy combination!

Being a parent never came that naturally to him, which is not to say he wasn't a great dad, I wouldn't have changed him for the world, but he did struggle with the emotional side of things, almost certainly because he'd never received any compassion from his own parents. So, we didn't get much in the way of hugs and kisses or that much in the way of approval from him, but this was ok, we had our mum for that side of things. We did receive a big cuddle every New Year which was priceless.

I know he loved us unconditionally, he just showed it in different ways. To put it simply, there was nothing he wouldn't do for his family. From a young age I played table tennis to a decent standard. Having worked a fifty-hour week, most weekends dad would take me to tournaments all over the country. We were often setting off as early as four in the morning and not getting back home until late Sunday evenings. We've never been what you'd call well off and consequently, we've stopped in some dodgy bedsits over the years, but he always found a way to get me to all the main events. Even though I know that deep down he had little to no interest in the sport. All he ever stipulated was that the guesthouse had a bar. As long as this was the case, he wouldn't moan about anything. We could drag him off to anywhere in the country. I'd like to think that he enjoyed some of our weekends away, especially twice a year when we got to go to Blackpool. Mum would come with us and we would stay in the same little hotel on the sea front. Dad particularly liked this one because there was always a live music act on and he loved nothing more than listening, whilst unwinding with a pint in his hand. It was always great seeing him so relaxed and contented.

When he wasn't away with me, he spent much of his spare time watching my brother play cricket. This involved sitting on the sidelines, in often freezing conditions, and cricket can be a long game! If he knew it was important to us, then it would be important to him too. He showed amazing commitment to his family.

Dad had no time for misbehaving kids; in fact, they frustrated the hell out of him. He would soon lose his patience and blame the parents. He put it down to lack of discipline and found it unforgivable when they failed to control their kids. In his eyes there was no excuse for this. In contrast when we were out with our parents we always behaved impeccably. If in a pub or restaurant, we would sit quietly and not move a muscle until we were given permission. Whether out on a bus or in a supermarket shopping, whilst other kids were screaming and being disruptive, we would remain quiet and as good as gold.

Other parents would be fascinated by this and often stare in disbelief. This was completely down to dads influence over us. Although he never smacked us, he had a certain presence, a way of looking at us that would immediately demand his respect. Due to this, we were terrified of the consequences of misbehaving, especially in public.

As long as we stuck to his rules, he was actually a lot of fun. I have many happy childhood memories of him playing in parks with us, taking us swimming and clowning around on the beach on family holidays.

Dad saw Christmas, as another chance to show us how much he loved us, he always managed to make it a magical time. Even working on a tight budget, we were always spoilt with sacks full of presents. He embraced the opportunity to bring the whole family together for a big slap-up meal. We would all wear party hats, pull crackers, and play silly games, and he would relish being the host.

As a child I wasn't always able to relate to my dad, but I always felt greatly protected by him.

It's only as I grew up into adulthood that our relationship became much stronger. We discovered we were very much on the same wavelength and had the same dry sense of humour. We both took high delight in winding my brother up, especially about his beloved Manchester Utd. He used to refer to us as Laurel and Hardy, as we were like a comedy duo. I'd prefer to think of us as two peas in a pod.

I was able to see him in a completely different light as he used to take me to the club for a pint and a game of snooker. This soon became our Saturday teatime ritual. After a few beers he would let his guard down and I got to see glimpses of a more sensitive side. Every year in the weeks surrounding Christmas, I would become his drinking buddy in the house as well. He would wait for my mum and brother to go to bed and then he'd say, "night cap son?" and get the whisky bottle out. I'd ask for a small measure, but he'd ignore this and pour me a tumbler full, saying "don't be daft son, it's Christmas" it was round about now that the philosophical dad would come out. He would look up at the night sky and start musing about how vast the universe was and pondering where we all came from. I learnt how fascinated he was with all the stars.

This was a special time that just dad and I shared, and these are the memories that will always be most precious to me.

As I've already said, sentiment didn't come easy to him, but the day I gave a best man speech at my friend's wedding, was the one time he took me to one side and told me how proud he was. He said that I'd done an incredible job and done something he could never have managed himself. To get this recognition from my dad was priceless. I'm sure there were many other occasions that he was proud of me, but he didn't find it easy to say. That's why I will always cherish that moment.

Looking back, there's so much about him that makes me smile, but I'll try to sum it up briefly.

He was one of the most honest people I knew, he would tell people exactly what he thought, whether they were ready for it or not! This painful honesty could at times be construed as tactless, but at least you knew where you stood with him.

In over thirty years of marriage, I never heard him, and my mum have a cross word with each other. He hated Valentine's Day. He always said it was far too commercial, but he would make up for it the rest of the year, he loved to spoil her and would do so with constant romantic gestures.

Even though he liked to adopt a tough guy demine he was secretly a big softy at heart. This was most evident with his love/hate relationship with Patch, our family cat, who he claimed he had no time for, but then when none of us was around, he'd have her sat on his knee and she'd be contentedly purring away.

As a child my brother broke his leg. He was given exercise regimes to assist with his recovery. Every night dad would get home from work and take him to the local swimming baths to help him with his exercises. Over time he could visibly see improvements, as the leg began to strengthen, until eventually he was able to walk again.

If my dad were still around today, I think he'd find my illness extremely difficult to comprehend. He hated seeing any of his family suffering, but I think he would especially struggle with the fact that with depression there is no obvious fix, and he wouldn't have known how to help.

Right up until the end of his life dad was still protecting us. He didn't want us to see him ill in a hospital bed. He made my mum promise to keep us away.

It's a testament to his character that even when in pain and at his most vulnerable, he was still able to put his family first.

A BRIEF GLIMPSE INTO FARTHERHOOD

Much of what happens in life can be cruelly influenced by timing. One of my work relationships was with a girl called Liz. She had a sweet selfless nature, was beautifully innocent and could be wonderfully weird at times. At first, every time she entered the room, I became a stuttering wreck. I had got it bad! But once I got over the initial butterflies in my stomach, I mustered the courage to ask her out. We were only together for six months, but this was long enough for me to realise she was the girl for me, someone I imagined growing old with. Although she was very fond of me, sadly she didn't feel the same way. As you might imagine, I was left heartbroken.

The only reason I've brought this up, is because prior to this, I'd had a three-year relationship with a girl called Carla. We were friends first, until things matured into something more. However, I never felt the same kind of spark, as I was to later have with Liz. In an ideal world if I had felt the same way, I may well have found everything I'd ever wanted. You see, Carla had a three-year-old son who I became extremely fond of. I was shocked by this, as I'd never been great with kids, and the thought of getting involved with someone who had one, was a scary prospect to say the least. But amazingly, we got on great right from the start and it wasn't too long before he was calling me daddy. Despite of him not being mine we grew very close, and he became my little buddy. When he used to fall and hurt himself, I'd be there to pick him up and tell him what a brave boy he was. I used to carry him up to his bed on an evening when he fell asleep on the couch. I'd get up in the night with him when he'd had a bad dream, reassure him that everything would be alright, and sit with him for as long as he needed me. From winning the egg and spoon race at his school sports day, to appearing as a shepherd in his first nativity play, whenever he achieved something, I would feel immense pride. It's impossible to spend three years with a child who dotes on your every word, without forming such a strong emotional attachment, like I did. I appreciate that it might not be the same as with your own child, but it might well be the closest I ever come. I still developed the same parental instincts and still felt an overwhelming protection towards him.

The reality is, his mother and I were never going to be forever. If it wasn't for the child, we may have split up much sooner. Looking back, I think I was more in love with the idea of a readymade family. As much as I liked Carla, I wasn't in love with her. She decided that continuing my relationship with her son would be too confusing for him and would potentially hurt him more. Saying goodbye to him was one of the hardest things I've ever done. When he realized what was happening, he grabbed hold of my leg to try and stop me from leaving. This agonizing image has remained with me, even though 19 years have passed, not having a chance to see him grow up will always be one of my biggest regrets.

FRIEND OR FOE

I took a week off work for bereavement. I was very conscious of the fact; I'd only been in the job for 6 months and I didn't want to take any liberties. The truth is, I thought I was ready to return, but it soon became apparent that I wasn't. It was growing increasingly difficult, to do what was already an emotionally demanding job. Somehow, I lasted a further 6 months.

During this time, I dreaded every shift and had to force myself to go in. I began drinking more heavily every evening, in an attempt to switch off and get some sleep.

To be honest, even though I claim that I like a drink, surprisingly, I've never really enjoyed the taste that much. However, I do like the way it makes me feel (most of the time), and I can't deny, it's played a significant role in my life.

I know it's said to be a depressant, but the truth is some of my happiest memories spent with friends, have involved alcohol. On the flip side of this, when I think back to my saddest, most despondent moments in life, I tend to have a drink in my hand. I can be extremely shy, especially around the opposite sex.

Without alcohol in my life, I doubt if I'd have ever had a girlfriend. You see, without a few drinks or nerve settlers as I call them, I'd have never had the courage to approach someone, let alone tell them that I liked them. It's true what they say, it does help you lose your inhibitions. I genuinely believe that it helps me become a more interesting person. I realise that must sound ridiculous, as I'm still the same person. But with it, I feel more outgoing and much less self-conscious. I can even look in the mirror without noticing all my flaws. When in a group, I'm able to contribute to the conversations without feeling out of place as I normally would.

There's nothing worse than bringing your work home with you, but I had great difficulty switching off at the end of my shifts. Added to this, I was struggling to come to terms with the loss of my father. Alcohol helped me to de-stress and guaranteed me getting at least a few hours' sleep. The trouble is it was never what you'd call a satisfying sleep. I'd often wake up feeling groggy and even more tired than when I'd gone to bed. At what stage would I have to admit, it was becoming an issue? Over time the 3 cans of lager that used to be sufficient, was having little to no effect. Soon 3 became 4, and then 4 became 5. Before I knew it, I was having 6 strong beers a night, followed by a couple of whisky chasers. Sometimes I didn't make it up to bed, instead I'd find myself comatosed on the sofa. I never woke up feeling refreshed, I never felt well at all. At work I'd go through all the motions but find it hard to concentrate on anything other than getting home for my next drink. One young man who attended my drop-in groups regularly, worked as a hospital porter. He claimed that the only way he could switch off on an evening, was to have 4 pints before going to bed. He asked me once if I considered him to be an alcoholic. I can't remember my exact response, but how could I give him any constructive advice, when I was doing the exact same thing!

The definition of alcoholism is a condition in which dependence on alcohol harms a person's health and everyday life. For sure, I had become dependent on it and for sure, it was having a detrimental effect on my life. I recognised this and worked hard to change things. I needed to put my own health first, and I did this firstly, by quitting my job. Under much duress I went to see my doctor. He was concerned about my state of mind and decided that I needed anti-depressants, and that I'd benefit from some grief counselling.

The trouble with having an addictive personality, is it's far too easy to fall back into bad habits. I'm careful and guard against this happening. I still like a drink, but I must be disciplined and enjoy it in moderation. I won't lie to you, I do slip up occasionally, but I mostly stick to my ground rules. When I'm having a drink at home my limit is 3 beers and I try not to drink 2 nights consecutively. If I'm feeling sad, I try to accept that drinking will only make me feel worse. Presently, I can't drink more than a couple without becoming sick, as alcohol doesn't mix well with my medication.

You might consider my past reliance to be a bit alarming, but many people use it as a crutch. How is insisting on having a glass of wine with your evening meal any different? As for the question of friend or foe? I think the jury's still out on that one. One thing I do accept is it can quickly get out of hand and therefore I must remain careful.

PANIC ATTACKS

Ever since I can remember I've been an anxious person, apparently, even as a young child I appeared more apprehensive than most other kids. I've been told, that at nursery school I would go into complete meltdown every time I was asked to choose my own toy to play with, hardly a life altering decision, I know, but I'd much rather be told where to sit and what to do, than have to make the choices for myself. It's therefore not that surprising that I would have stress related issues later in my life.

As I've already alluded to, high school was a difficult time and certainly a large contributing factor, but all that aside, I didn't start suffering with panic attacks until a much later date.

After leaving my career in mental health, for the reasons I shared in the last chapter, I had a few temporary jobs, before finally getting a permanent position in a small care home, looking after people with learning disabilities and challenging behaviours, at the time I had no idea how severe these behaviours were or how I was likely to respond to them. For the first two weeks I was away from the home taking part in mandatory training. Ninety-five percent of which involved learning how to defend yourself and how to safely restrain people who were trying to cause you harm. By the end of the fortnight my body was already battered and bruised, just from the staff role-play and I was feeling decidedly uneasy about my first shift.

I remember trying to convince myself that it wouldn't be that bad, that the training was only showing the worst-case scenarios. This didn't stop me anticipating a nightmare, and a nightmare is exactly what I got. I lasted less than two more weeks and during this time I had some truly horrendous shifts, shifts which have stuck, in my memory.

On my very first day the staff locked me in the kitchen for my own protection! Whilst in there, what seemed like world war three was breaking out in the rest of the home. People were shouting and screaming, furniture and chairs were being thrown around. At one point I heard an earth-shattering crash, which turned out to be the television smashing against the wall. I remember thinking what the hell am I doing here.

Later that day one of the residents was kind enough to spit in my face and tell me he wished I were dead. This was new for me; I'd worked in care for a long time and never had anyone take such an instant dislike to me.

One thing that was repeated several times in training, was that, if you were ever alone in a room with a resident, always make sure you positioned yourself closest to the exit. Towards the end of my first week, I made the cardinal mistake of forgetting this advice. In a desperate attempt to build some report with one of the residents, I went to look at his video collection at the far end of his bedroom. I was really pleased that I'd finally found a way to relate to him, but in doing this I stupidly put myself in a vulnerable position. Before I could react, he had his arm across my chest and was slamming me into his bookshelf, it took two members of staff to prize him off me. I came out of it quite lucky, with just a small graze to my back but as you can imagine, such a violent incident did shake me up. As bad as it felt, I recognised that it was my own careless fault and that I could have avoided it happening. This made it easier for me to accept, I would just have to be more careful in the future.

The final incident upset me more than anything had so far and turned out to be the final straw. Even though all the residents were in the home due to their challenging behaviour, the youngest called Damien really stood out to me. He was autistic and had more severe learning disabilities than the other residents. He lived in his own little fantasy world where his favourite cartoon characters were his best friends. He was much like the people I had previously cared for. We immediately hit it off and he responded well to me. I felt sorry for him though, he appeared very young and vulnerable in this environment. That is why I found this incident most unsettling. It all started when somebody broke the glass that sets the fire alarm off, which apparently was a regular occurrence. At the time I was sat in the dining room with Damien, having helped him to make himself a sandwich. On hearing the alarm, he became extremely agitated. Before I knew it, he had thrown and smashed his plate against the wall and was storming out of the room. I hurried after him but didn't catch him in time, as he went into the lounge and slapped one of the girls hard across the face. She was just sat on a couch minding her own business at the time. I couldn't believe what I was witnessing, it was like someone had flipped a switch in his head.

Inevitably, the situation escalated as the other residents began to lose their temper. The boss had me take Damien to his room and lock the door for our own safety. But the truth is I didn't feel safe, this young man who I'd earlier felt sorry for, was not that innocent after all. During the whole incident I felt powerless and I'm ashamed to say I completely froze. I handed my notice in at the end of the shift and didn't return.

Shortly after this I got another job in care, working in a day center, very similar to what I'd done before, I even knew some of the service users. This should have been a comfortable job for me, but in the end, I didn't even last the morning. All of a sudden, I couldn't be a carer anymore. I had lost all my trust in people, literally everyone seemed like a potential threat, and I was convinced I was going to get attacked. The fact that there was a door code for the safety of the members, was also a big issue. Suddenly I was back to being locked in again, trapped. I felt like the walls were coming in on me and that there were far too many people for such a small space. My chest began to tighten, and I couldn't breathe. It was very strange; I could see staff members were talking to me, but I wasn't able to hear a word they were saying. By now my heart felt like it was beating out of my chest and I was gasping for air. All that was important, was that I got out, I didn't care how ridiculous I looked, I was just desperate to escape. I frantically tried to open the door, but I hadn't been given the code yet! I've never felt so small in all my life; I've never felt so afraid, I was certain I was going to die. This was the first time I had a panic attack.

Gradually over the coming years my anxiety levels worsened, the attacks became more frequent and much more random. Taking place in shops and supermarkets, on public transport and in many other social situations.

Even in my own home I would panic about having to answer the telephone, not knowing who was on the other end of the line. I soon became fearful of opening my mail.

Having a panic attack is a terrifying experience and one that I now try to avoid at any cost. This can quickly result in not wanting to leave the house, feelings of inadequacy, severe confidence problems and soon lead to a deep depression. Eventually I got to the stage where I couldn't function properly, and all these irrational fears were becoming disruptive to my life.

It's amazing how quickly things can spiral out of control. You rapidly go from nervous or a little anxious, to totally neurotic. You might not even realise it's happening to you, as strange as that sounds. In my case it was family who made me aware of all my avoidance behaviour. I genuinely didn't know how long I'd been in isolation for, or how long it had been since I'd interacted with someone outside of the household.

PANIC ATTACKS – A terrifying sudden dread which soon escalates into breathing difficulties, chest pain, disorientation, and a genuine fear of death.

ANXIETY/STRESS- Irrational thoughts, over thinking, hopelessness.

AVOIDANCE BEHAVIOUR- Never leaving the house, canceling plans with friends, lying constantly to get out of things.

LOW SELF-ESTEEM- Major confidence issues and insecurities. A Self-loathing side that brings all your inadequacies to the forefront and leaves you feeling useless.

DEPRESSION- Fed up, lack of motivation, lack of energy. Days become torturous and you feel like giving up on life.

Panic attacks can lead to Depression and Depression can lead right back to Panic attacks. You soon find yourself in a vicious cycle, that becomes extremely damaging to your mental health.

Before I continue with my story, in the next chapter I'm going to share a little about what it's like to live with social anxiety.

SOCIAL ANXIETY

Is it possible that the elderly couple at the bus stop are just simply waiting for the bus? Why then do I view them as such a great threat, why do I genuinely believe them to be carrying weapons! So much so that I must cross over the road to get past.

Is it possible that the work van parked on the corner of my street, is just parked up whilst the work man has his lunch break? Why then do I think He's waiting for me to walk past so he can bundle me into the back and kidnap me! so much so that I must find a much longer alternative route.

I see a garage door slightly open, light on in the garage. Is it possible they're doing some work and want a bit of fresh air, maybe they've simply forgotten to close the door? But that's not what goes through my head, instead I convince myself that someone's in there spying on passers-by and they're going to jump out and attack me! Again, I can't risk walking past and so I find an alternative route.

Later when I'm sat at home, I feel foolish and embarrassed that I've reacted in this way, but it's hard to stop, as at the time the threat seems very real and very frightening!

My depression and anxiety lead to me having many irrational thoughts. I'm going to share with you a passage from my journal I composed a few months back. At the time we had workmen in the house fitting a new bathroom, my worst nightmare! Things like this badly affect me. My home is usually my safe zone but having strangers in it for any length of time changes things dramatically. It leads to me being petrified to move from room to room. Strategically planning my toilet trips, in a desperate attempt to avoid running into anyone. I'm left feeling like an intruder in my own home!

I went away with my mum for a few days, but when we returned, the work was nowhere near complete. Worst still, on the Monday it was mums volunteer morning at the hospice, and I was going to be left alone. I decided the lesser of two evils was to go with her. I didn't like the prospect of sitting in a room full of folks having to make conversation, but it was better than the alternative of getting under the work men's feet. Here's word for word what I wrote at the time.

At least the suns shining, it's not such a bad day to die if this is to be my time. That's what was going through my mind 10 minutes ago, walking down the road from the Kirkwood hospice, with potential threats to my life at either side of me. I wasn't scared but at the same time felt distinctly uneasy, who am I kidding, I was petrified! I just prayed that if this were my time, it would be over quickly and relatively painlessly, maybe a swift knife to the chest or something along those lines!

I'm now sat in a café, I feel uncomfortable and extremely self-conscious, but at least it's safe in here. Safer than out there anyway! As usual I have picked a spot in the darkest dingiest corner, as far away from prying eyes as possible. This will be ok for the next three hours. It turned out I couldn't stay in the hospice with all those people, and I couldn't stay at home either! so here I am in the middle of plan C. It's not ideal, I haven't been out on my own for this long for some time and I'm feeling very vulnerable. Writing this is passing time and if I can somehow keep hidden for another hour, I'll attempt to walk back. The world is a scary place and I'm not equipped to cope. I wish I were normal; I wish I weren't such a freak!

Another problem just occurred to me. I need the toilet and I'm going to have to walk past a table of students to get there. Oh my God, what am I going to do now! Maybe I'll be able to hold on until they've gone, I'll have too, there's no way I'm walking past them! How ridiculous, I think I'd rather wet myself than walk past these people, and let's face it, they're probably to engrossed in their conversations to even notice me!

Somehow, I've managed to get back to the hospice unscathed, and bravely come in to join the group. I've even found a corner seat again. Maybe if I keep my head down writing folks might leave me alone. Evidently there's 40 people in the room, to me it feels more like 400!

At the time of writing this book the world is in the verge of fighting a pandemic called the coronavirus. Like many other countries, ours (the UK), has been placed in lockdown, as the fatalities continue to rise. Rightly or wrongly, our government has been quite lenient on the restrictions. Were as other countries are being much stricter on the penalties for people flaunting the rules. However, social distancing is being adhered to by most. Due to my anxiety, I don't like being around too many people anyway. For years I have become a master of self-isolation, not leaving the house for long periods of time has become the norm. when I do risk going outside, it's natural for me to give folks a wide birth. All the recommendations the government have given, such as crossing the road to avoid close contact with people, I've been doing for years. I don't have to change my routine in the slightest. For other people, lack of social interaction is tough. They rely heavily on it, and after just a couple of weeks, they're climbing the walls with boredom! To these people, I say, welcome to my world! Imagine fearing to leave your house and having these feelings of shear dread every single day for years to come. Only then, will you get what it's truly like to self-isolate. Some have it tougher than me, their homes become their prison, the only fresh air they get is through the window. I can at least get out some of the time.

I've stopped pegging the washing out on a weekend, for fear of encountering the neighbours. This is ridiculous as we have good neighbours, they're perfectly pleasant and really shouldn't cause me any trepidation what so ever. However, the prospect of having a two-minute chat with them (probably about the weather!) to pass the time of day is so horrifying, that I simply can't risk it.

Sadly my avoidance tactics don't stop there, as my social anxiety starts to get the better of me. Getting the wheelie bin from the side of the house, once a week on its collection day, has quite frankly become a military operation. I tend to do it the night before when it's dark and I'm less likely to be seen. I have to look out of the front, back and side windows before I even contemplate stepping outside. I open the back door ever so slightly and listen for a minute or two, then tentatively, I stick my head out and check both ways. Only when I'm completely satisfied that no ones around, will I make my move. If this was an Olympic event I'd win gold every time, I literally have it done in a flash, like my life depends on it, then I'm back in the safety of my house, taking a few deep breaths and thanking God I don't have to do it again for another week.

I began to lose my hair at a young age and by my early twenties there wasn't much left. Since then I have always cut it myself, and like to keep it shaved very short.

That was until six months a go when my clippers broke. As you've probably gathered by now, I don't do social interaction too well. Hairdressers are notorious for being the chattiest of all people. Sometimes sitting in that chair for ten minutes can feel like hours. I find it torturous to say the least, as they delve into your life history! Therefore, I saw this as an ideal opportunity to challenge myself by taking myself out of my comfort zone. This is roughly how it went:

Barbers number 1- Cheerful enough but far too talkative. Constant questions tripping off his tongue, including asking what I did for a living, a subject which makes me feel uncomfortable at the best of times.

Barbers number 2- This one was disturbing. She was fascinated by the heat coming from my head, so much so she got the other hairdressers to come across and have a feel! This left me feeling self-conscious to say the least, and I couldn't wait to escape.

Barbers number 3- This one couldn't understand why I didn't cut my own hair. I told him that it was only temporary until I got some new clippers. As soon as I said that I realised I wouldn't be able to return. Not that I would have anyway, he was far too chatty for my liking!

Barbers number 4- This one was interesting, nowhere near as friendly as the others. All the customers and staff seemed to know each other and this created a strange atmosphere. When I walked in, everyone appeared to stop what they were doing and stare at me like I didn't belong in their company. Like a scene from an old western as a newcomer enters the saloon. Hardly the most welcoming of places!

Barbers number 5- Ran by a Turkish family, I finally found the perfect place for me, where the staff only understood a little English and couldn't speak more than two words of it. When it was your turn they'd point to the chair and say, "sit". When finished they'd say "five pounds" and that's the only bit of chitchat I had to endure. Absolutely ideal! And this is the one I've chosen to return too.

I accept that people may view me as a bit of a party pooper and some are probably sick of inviting me to places- only for me to come up with yet more excuses! I can put up with being branded antisocial. But when did I get to the stage were I had this constant feeling of inadequacy? As my self-doubt reaches it's peak, I start to view myself as a huge burden and believe that people deserve a medal for putting up with me. I need to remind myself that this is not true. How I deal with these difficult emotions is crucial. Presently, I choose to look at the funny side of my social anxiety. Learning to laugh at yourself is such an important coping tool. You put less emphasis on your frailties, there not that important, there just something you can laugh about. Suddenly, you find you have less anxiety moving forwards. Unfortunately, I havent always been able to do this. I've always been far better at giving advice than taking it.

Over the next few years my mental health got a great deal worse. I wasn't able to work anymore, due to my severe anxiety, an anxiety of which I didn't fully understand. I shut myself away for lengthy periods. During these times i refused to communicate with anyone. I did attend the job centre, signing on for a while, but after having a full blown panic attack and ending up in a heap on the floor, this too became an impossibility. I decided that I'd rather live without benefits all together than put myself through this process. I'll talk more about the benefit system later in the book. In 2015 I finally reached breaking point.

A GENTLE BREEZE

Imagine being engulfed in a deep fog, not sure where you're going, or if you'll ever get there. Trudging through a thick unforgiving sludge. The harder you try, the further you sink. Every aching muscle in your body is crying out for you to give up. The days become a chore, as your body gets heavier and the pressure valve increases, it becomes increasingly difficult to breathe. Welcome to the life of a depressant!

I was unmotivated and just couldn't see the point anymore. Even though I was desperate not to feel this way, I couldn't help it. I was fighting a losing battle and was left both perplexed and terrified by this. I felt lost and completely alone, even whilst in company. Swallowed up by a sickening sadness and sense of hopelessness. As the self-loathing voice inside my head became relentless, I was left battered and exhausted. In these moments I began to hate everything about myself. Even the simplest task became a huge effort, useless or inadequate are words that would spring to mind! It would be cruel to inflict my misery on others, and so, I chose isolation. Unfortunately, this gave me more time to dwell, which was a dangerous thing! Led on my bed I found it hard to lift my head from the pillow, and soon the pain and inward torment became overwhelming. For hours on end, staring at the same spot on the ceiling. Pretty soon I found myself wishing I were dead!

In 2015, I came perilously close to taking my life for the first time. I was in an extremely dark place and the pain and mental anguish I was experiencing, was far too much to handle. I didn't fully understand why I was feeling this way, which made it all so much harder. Even though I'd been seeing a counsellor for some time, asking for help on this was not an option, I was far too ashamed and didn't feel deserving of it. I felt like I'd become a burden to everyone important in my life. I genuinely believed that killing myself was the only option left.

And so, I began putting plans in place for after I'd gone. I wrote personal letters to each of my loved ones, cleared all my debts and left enough in the bank to pay for my funeral. I even put a list together of telephone numbers my family would need to contact after my death. I really gave it a lot of thought and attempted to cover all angles.

Shortly after this I took myself to the spot where I intended to do the deed, a nearby quarry with a massive drop, easily deep enough for the job. I wasn't sure if today would be the day or if it were just to be a practice run (as ridiculous as this must sound!) Much of my memory of this is still a bit hazy, but I do recall it being a cloudy but fine day, I can't remember much of the walk up, but I found myself stood on the edge. I closed my eyes and thought about how easy it would be. One simple step forward and my problems would be over, the pain would finally stop.

For months, I'd asked myself the same question **'am I enough?'** And I'd basically concluded that I wasn't, that I had nothing left to offer. I mean, what possible right or reason did I have to be depressed? Having such amazing friends and such a supportive family, somehow made it worse. It left me with a terrible guilt and unbearable shame. My life was a car crash. Any forlorn attempt to change things had proved unsuccessful, there was an inevitability that it would all lead to this point.

I'd just about convinced myself that today was going to be the day, one step, that's all it would take. But then a strange sensation came over me. I was suddenly greeted by a warm breeze against my forehead. It felt good. It felt strangely comforting. I opened my eyes to see the sun breaking through the cloud and lighting up the whole valley. It was almost as if the world had gone into slow motion. What a stunning view, I couldn't believe I hadn't noticed it before! I broke down, overwhelmed with emotion. Today wasn't to be the day after all.

Later I confided in my counsellor, sharing my entire plan with her. At this point she made me get the extra help I needed. I was still adamant I was going to end my life and put it down to shear cowardice that I hadn't done it already. Over time she helped me see that not taking my life, was in fact the bravest thing I'd ever done. The help that I've received since that day has been invaluable. The reality is, I'm nowhere near recovered, I may never be. But I have learnt to manage my illness much better. Some days I find myself very down and too anxious to leave the house on my own, it still feels like I'm surviving at best! But all this aside, it's rare that I wake up dreading the day, instead I find myself looking forward to things to come.

COUNSELLING

Over the years I've become a master of repressing my feelings. Bottling up my emotions has always seemed the best and safest option, therefore it's become the norm.

I think much of this stems from the fear of being out of control. If I allow myself to cry, I might not be able to stop. I've come to realise that shutting all your issues away like this does not overcome them, they will still be there, and as they mount up, the pressure also builds, before long you become desperate for some kind of release. I recognised I needed help and so, with the help of my doctor, I got myself on a list to see a counsellor. In the hope they might be able to delve a bit deeper and hopefully get to the root of my problems.

The therapy I received over an 18-month period, had been surprisingly beneficial. I say this because being a cynical person, I had little to no expectations of it helping whatsoever. In the rest of this chapter, I'll share some of my journey with you, which saw me going from dreading the mere thought of having to talk about myself for a full hour, to the stage where I actually looked forward to and gained strength from my sessions. Often then, an hour didn't seem long enough, and I was left feeling disappointed when Nancy told me our time was coming to an end.

Going back to the beginning.

I started the process very tentatively, I found it extremely difficult to bear my sole to a total stranger. I also felt undeserving of the help, like there were people much more in need than me, and like I was potentially taking up their space.

For the first few weeks I was very defensive, I was looking for hidden agendas in everything Nancy said to me. I spent half of the time attempting to convince her I was ok and the other half apologising for being there.

Even though I referred myself to the service and did this because I knew, deep down I needed the help, I still found myself trying all sorts of distraction techniques to avoid having to talk about what were extremely difficult emotions. I'd try to use humour as a defense mechanism and frequently attempted to change the subject or get her to talk about herself. Unfortunately for me, Nancy was too good at her job to ever fall for these tactics. The truth is, she never divulged any personal information, meaning I knew as little about her now as I did from the beginning.

This, as well as being professional, was a clever way of ensuring the whole session was concentrated solely around me. I have to admit this took a while to get used to, I've never liked being the centre of attention. If possible, I much prefer to blend into the background. In counselling I wasn't afforded this luxury. I was encouraged to be honest and speak my mind, however bad I was feeling.

I always felt I had to balance a negative by immediately giving a positive, it's something I do less now but I'm still guilty of. At the start, I did it to protect myself, as being in a vulnerable state felt very uncomfortable. As well as this I didn't think it was fair to burden Nancy with too much heavy stuff all at once. I now realise she was more than equipped to handle it. Over time I found myself apologising less for my negative emotions.

In counselling sessions, you have to be prepared to be stripped bare (Figurately speaking). To share some of your inner most feelings takes time and only works if you have complete trust in your counsellor. It took me five months before I got to this stage. This might sound like a long time but with my trust issues, it's a miracle I found anyone I could talk to at all. Once I began sharing things, suddenly everything just started pouring out of me. I was able to be completely honest, including talking about my suicidal thoughts, and the quarry plan that I almost carried out. Just to be able to tell someone that I didn't want to be here anymore was a massive relief.

Nancy had created an environment where I felt completely safe and able to share whatever was on my mind. Every time I got something off my chest, it felt like a huge weight had been lifted. I was able to leave all my negative energy behind me in the room and start a fresh. We always worked towards achieving this goal.

Throughout the process, there were times when I found it easier to write down how I was feeling, rather than say it out loud. Nancy encouraged me to write, some weeks she even set me homework! One such time, she asked me to describe what I saw when I looked in the mirror. This is exactly what I came up with at the time.

When I look in the mirror, I see lots of things, surprisingly! It's hard to get past the initial thought of hating the way I look, with big bags under my eyes, dry flaky skin, spots everywhere, bald on top making me look at least ten years older!

But when I look a bit deeper, the main thing I see is sadness. I try to mask it with a smile, but it looks awkward and forced. In the end it's my haunted looking eyes that give me away. One minute I look like a frightened little boy with all the troubles of the world on my shoulders. The next time

I look, I see nothing, emptiness, a distant blank expression. Maybe my defense mechanism is to completely switch off, or maybe I'm seeing someone who has lost all hope and is slowly giving up on life. Either way this vulnerable person staring back at me both scares and disappoints me.

I'm pleased to say that at present my perceptions have somewhat changed. I'm not about to insult your intelligence by saying I've miraculously gone from hating my appearance, to suddenly liking it, because that's simply not true. I have noticed some subtle changes though, that have made observing myself a little more bearable.

Whereas before, I saw emptiness, fear, and confusion, now I see more understanding and even glimpses of optimism.

It's perfectly normal to see all your flaws, especially when you're studying yourself so intently. Even the most beautiful people will still find things they're not happy with if they look hard enough. We are our own worse critics after all.

How easy is it to stand in front of a full-length mirror working your way from head to toe, highlighting all the things you're not happy with? Tiny blemishes can soon get magnified into hideous deformities. Of course, these are only visible to you and not to others around you. In fact, some of the time, what you view as an imperfection, someone else might find to be an attractive feature. What I would picture as tired, beaten up, sad eyes with big bags under them, have been described by my ex-girlfriends as warm and friendly or even gorgeous come to bed eyes! Equally there have been things about themselves that they have disliked and become paranoid over, things which I have genuinely found to be most endearing. The trouble is most of us don't take compliments too well, and don't always believe them to be true. I can take a lot of convincing, when someone finds something about me attractive, something that I've only ever viewed as being ugly.

In conclusion, what you see in yourself is often a totally different person than what others see in you. I am guilty of attaching too much importance to every little flaw I find, which as we've discussed might not even be seen like this, in other people's eyes.

Everyone is unique, we all come in various shapes and sizes and we're all attracted to different qualities in each other. As humans we are such a diverse group, it's pointless putting too much emphasis on how we look, as I honestly believe there's somebody out there for everyone.

All this of course is much easier to put down on paper than to put into practice. The reality is, I still have issues with my body image, which unfortunately continues to have a negative effect on me.

However, I am now able to look at myself in the mirror without experiencing the same discomfort as previously.

'Our problem is that we make the mistake of comparing ourselves with other people. You are not inferior or superior to any human being... You don't determine your success by comparing yourself to others, rather you determine your success by comparing your accomplishments to your capabilities. You are 'number one' when you do the best you can with what you have' (Zig Siglar- American motivational writer)

At some stage in the counselling process, Nancy had seen me in every imaginable state. From total despondency and desperation, to being upbeat and optimistic, I no longer held back with my emotions. When I'm at my pessimistic best, I must be very difficult to work with, but she always found a way. There are still times when I'm extremely insecure and require lots of patience and reassurance. When I'm like this, I need someone to be considerate and show me copious amounts of empathy and understanding. On the flip side of this, there's times when I need a foot up my arse! Someone to motivate and challenge me to do more, pushing myself further.

Nancy was able to find the perfect blend of both and used the necessary approach, dependent on my mood. She was able to get her point across subtly, without ramming it down my throat.

We had a strong connection that developed from trust and honesty. She now knows personal things about me that even my closest friends don't know. Even though I knew very little about her, I knew enough, which was that she genuinely cared about my welfare. We also seemed to be on the same wavelength and have a similar sense of humour, which of course made things easier. Often when I turned up at my sessions, she'd have researched information for me that she believed might be useful. I know she didn't have to go that extra mile, but she chose to do so anyway, which again showed that she cared.

My counselling taught me to appreciate myself much more. It's also involved me getting to know a whole new side, which in the past I've neglected and shut away.

Counselling completely altered my outlook; it's helped me to realise that my illness is nothing to be ashamed of. This in turn has contributed to me involving more people. I now find it much easier to open up to friends and family and this is far less stressful than the alternative of hiding behind elaborate excuses, like I've done in the past.

It's such a relief to finally be honest about the way I'm feeling, and I've been pleasantly surprised by the responses I get. All though not everyone gets it, the majority of people are understanding when it comes to mental health illness. I wonder now why I hid it for as long as I did. It would have been much healthier to have been more open right from the beginning.

After my suicide attempt, began an arduous journey. Starting about six months into my counselling, by asking for help, I 'd took a big step in the right direction, although it didn't feel this way at the time. Confiding in Nancy was a start, but now the hard work would begin. She thanked me for my honesty, but then explained that, if I wanted to continue seeing her (which I desperately needed to) I'd have to tell my doctor, in detail about my suicidal thoughts. This scared the hell out of me, I knew if he believed me to be a serious risk, there was a possibility

I could be sectioned for my own protection. To say I was worried about this, would be the understatement of the century! Having spent a small stint working on a mental health ward, I recognised, it wasn't an environment I could ever handle as a patient. So, I had to weigh up the risk, against my desire to continue with the counselling. I was angry with Nancy for putting me in this position. Right from the start, she had promised me a safe place, where, whatever I said would remain strictly confidential. It felt a bit like she'd betrayed me, I'd been encouraged to share my inner most feelings, and now, I was being punished for it. In reflection I can see that she had no choice, as she was following her strict professional guidelines. I also accept that she had my best interest at heart and that my anger towards her was born out of fear, rather than logical thinking.

I spoke to my doctor and didn't spare any details. When asked some in depth questions, I was brutally honest, saying that I considered suicide every day, and if it wasn't for the breeze at the top of the quarry, then I'd be dead already. He was genuinely concerned that I would leave the surgery and try again. I managed to convince him that all though I was still feeling bad, I had no immediate impulse to do this. Thankfully, he believed me and put things in place to try and help. He recommended that my counselling sessions should continue. My dosage of antidepressants was increased and the following day I had a home visit from the crisis team, who in turn registered me with a mental health team. Within a few weeks, I had my own community nurse, and a social worker who came to see me once a week. Shortly after this I got my own carer who would take me out and do graded exposure therapy (I'll explain more about this later in the book). I was also put on a list to see a psychologist. I had to maintain close communications with my doctor, having to attend appointments once a fortnight.

I couldn't believe the response. In fact, I was overwhelmed by it. One moment of complete honesty and I was receiving more help than royalty! To be honest, it all felt a tad surreal, almost like it was happening to somebody else.

Was I really worthy of all this support? Was it that bigger deal that I didn't want to be here anymore? Was I really depressed at all, or was I just weak minded and a waste of space? Accepting my illness was by far the hardest step for me, and speaking to most other sufferers, the same applied to them too.

ACCEPTANCE

Many people make the presumption that if you're depressed, you're bound to fall into a certain category. Maybe you've been disowned by your family, you've got no worthwhile friends to turn too and you're facing a life of solitary.

Maybe you have no outgoings, no reason to get up in a morning, nothing to be proud of and no purpose in life.

You might be financially unstable, facing bankruptcy, the bills are mounting up and you can't see an easy way out.

You might have a disability, which prevents you from living the life you want to live.

Or you might just be one of those people whose glass is always half empty, you somehow manage to find the negative side of every given situation and have a miserable outlook on life, which worse of all begins to rub off on everyone around you.

But what if none of these things apply to you, but you still find your world crumbling around you? I can honestly say that I have the best bunch of friends in the world, and I've been brought up in a loving family, which are still to this day amazingly supportive of me.

I have lots of hobbies and interests and enjoy many aspects of life.

I'd like to think of myself as a cheerful outgoing person and my friends would tell you that most of the time, I'm good company.

So, do I still have the right to be depressed?

Should I feel guilty for feeling the way I do, when I have such fantastic support all around me?

Well, the truth is I have felt extremely guilty and at times even disgusted with myself. I've certainly felt undeserving of any help.

In my career as a support worker, I spent much time caring for people who had multiple disabilities. Many of whom had limited movement of their limbs and spent much of their life's wheelchair bound. If ever anyone had the right to moan about life it was these people, yet they rarely did and on the contrary, had the most positive outlook. I found them truly inspiring. Every day on the news you see children being born into poverty and some being born into war zones. There are millions of people worse off than me, so what right or reason did I have to be depressed? As well as being confused and frustrated by the way I was feeling I also felt an unbearable shame and I was tormented by this for a long time to come.

Accepting my depression has been extremely difficult for me and I'm not certain I've quite got there yet. The truth is, I don't think it's an illness I'll ever fully understand. But it is an illness and a serious one at that, whether I believe myself to be worthy of it or not, I still have it and unfortunately that's completely out of my control. As much as I put myself down, I try to remember that I am a good person. The reason why I have so many great friends is because I too am a great friend. The reason why I have such a supportive family is because I am equally supportive of them. Right now, I need help and more to the point, I'm entitled to it.

Having spent most of my life caring for others and putting their needs first, why shouldn't I get a little help now?

The toughest part of all this for me was when I began to have suicidal thoughts. I was confused and in a state of total despondency. It's hard to describe but it's like suddenly being overwhelmed with sadness or engulfed in a never-ending darkness. Any motivation you have is completely depleted. You don't want to get out of bed and face your family, let alone leave the house to face the world.

I'd like to think I've always been a positive person, so I found these feelings both frightening and bewildering. At my lowest points, the thought of not being here anymore was and still is a comfort to me. I'm the sort of person who needed to, at least attempt to make sense of all this.

Another thing I took some convincing over was all the medication I'm now on. Previously even if I had a bad headache, I wouldn't take any painkillers for it. I just hated the thought of becoming reliant on tablets. Now I take three to six tablets a day including antidepressants, tablets to help me with my anxiety and sleeping pills. Before this year I had visited the doctors once in six years, now I have a regular fortnightly slot, how times have changed! I've got to admit I have a great doctor though; he's always been really understanding and will even let me sit outside in the car park if the waiting rooms to busy and there's any chance of me becoming overstressed. If he calls my name and I'm not there, he'll come out and get me. I shouldn't imagine many GP's offer this kind of service.

As for the medication, I'm getting used to it and I see it as a necessary short-term fix.

My major conflict has always been with myself and the constant arguments taking place in my head. This is not to say I'm in anyway psychotic or going insane! Everyone has at least two inner voices (you might have more, depending on your complexities!) and they can have a powerful influence over us. Every time you have a difficult decision to make, your opposing sides will kick into action. One part of you is the positive side that says 'I can do this' the other is the doubting or cautious side. This side of you is not necessarily that bad, sometimes it can benefit you, by being the voice of reason that keeps you safe.

In my case though, it's very obstructive. It likes to put me down, it's defeatist and critical of everything I try to do. Unhelpfully, it's also my noisiest side which often convinces me to take the wrong path. It's this side that made accepting my depression so difficult.

Daily, I find both my personas at loggerheads with each other. These constant disputes can be a heavy thing to carry around and become extremely tiresome. When I'm undecided if I can or can't do something, my self-doubting side grows more forceful and starts to take over, bringing all my insecurities to the forefront of my mind. Even if my optimistic side makes an appearance, it struggles to be heard over all the negativity. This nearly always results in me taking the cautious way out. The next time a similar situation arises, I feel more comfortable taking the 'I can't do this' approach, rather than the 'I can'. Before I know it, I'm accepting that I can't do very much at all! I become unwilling to take any risks whatsoever. All this achieves is me becoming more isolated and much more depressed.

I don't mean to overdramatize things, but the emotions going on in your head can be extremely powerful. In my case 'I can't' soon turns into 'No chance' or 'I'll never be able to' which leads to feelings of inadequacy and total worthlessness. Pretty soon, I'm at the stage where I can't see the point anymore and start to genuinely believe I'd be better off not here. If you've ever reached this level of anguish, then I feel very sorry for you. It's a horrible place to find yourself and a difficult one to escape from.

So, what's the answer? Is there any solution? Well, my solution was to surround myself with positive people, in the form of family and friends, and to accept the help that's out there, from different health care professionals. There's plenty of support available if you have the courage to ask for it. This all took time, but with the encouragement of all these great people, I finally began to turn a corner and head in the right direction. Although, far from well, I was getting a little stronger every day. I feel that dealing with my inner conflict helped me to accept my illness and tackle some big challenges still to come.

'Truly, it is in the darkness that one finds the light, so when we are in sorrow, then this light is nearest to

us. When it's dark enough, you can see the stars.'
(Johannes Eckhart)

The first step to recovery is accepting you have a problem in the first place. I know this is a clichéd statement overused in many self-help books, and by various therapists, but it is true. You can't possibly start attempting to fix something until you admit that it needs fixing in the first place.

Just like myself, you might be confused about your depression. There might not be an obvious reason for it; therefore, you can't see any immediate solution. There is plenty of support out there so try not to lose hope. Sometimes the hardest part can be asking for the help, but your GP's a good place to start.

There's also plenty you can do to help yourself and in the remainder of this book we will explore some of the coping tools that have been most useful to me. Before we do that though, I'd like to go back to my story.

After the events at the top of the quarry and the breeze that almost certainly saved my life, things started progressing quite quickly. I came to an abrupt realization, that I was very poorly, through no fault of my own. And that if I wanted to feel better, I'd have to accept some help.

It might sound strange, but I'd love to recreate the moments, both leading up to, and the few weeks after my suicidal attempt. I'll try and explain why in the next chapter.

NEGATIVE INTO POSITIVE

Rightly or wrongly, I took comfort from the thought of killing myself. Not so much the actual act but the idea of not being here anymore was very appealing.

I set the date for September, and in the build up to this, life somehow seemed much simpler. Both my counsellor and my doctor were always banging on about taking things one day at a time, which is good advice, I know, I just happen to hear it a lot! But now for the first time, I was actually able to put this into practice and stop worrying so much about the future. I knew that come September; I wouldn't have any future to worry about.

I didn't magically become a confident person overnight. I still had big issues with my anxiety. The difference was that when I had any fifty –fifty decisions to make, which I might have previously opted out of, now I would adopt the attitude of 'You might as well have a go'. I was going to die soon anyway, so what did I possibly have to lose! When I had convinced myself that I only had a few months left to live, bizarrely, I started to enjoy aspects of my life again.

It's a strange feeling and very hard to describe, but it's like suddenly, you become more appreciative of all the little things. Things that maybe in the past, you'd been guilty of taking for granted. Things like waking up from a satisfying sleep, enjoying a favourite meal or taking a nice scenic walk. Taking time to witness a clear starry night or a beautiful sunset. Time spent with friends becomes precious and much more meaningful.

The relief that I felt, allowed me to take a totally different outlook on life.

Much of my depression comes down to worrying about the future and what I think society expects of me. By that I mean, at 40 years old, I shouldn't be someone who's sponging off his mother and living off benefits.

Fortunately, people are becoming much more accepting of mental health being a serious illness and a legitimate reason, for me needing some extra support now. But what if I'm still like this a year or two years down the line? Will they still be as patient and understanding or are they more likely to become angry and resentful towards me. The truth is, I often feel angry and frustrated with myself. I have friends who are working forty to fifty-hour weeks to support their families and spending any spare time they have with their kids. Every time I see them, they look shattered. These are the people who deserve compassion, not me!

But then again, I didn't ask to be like this, did I? The trouble is I can't imagine getting to the stage where I'm not. I can't imagine ever being able to work a nine to five job again or having a family of my own. It's not that I'm not desperate to be that person, it's more a case I won't be able to handle it. The prospect of being responsible for anyone or anything, terrifies me. Let's face it; I'm finding it hard enough to take care of myself.

I used the thought of killing myself to my advantage, I somehow found a way to turn the ultimate negative into a positive. But when it went past September, and I was still here. I knew this should have been a reason to celebrate but instead, I was left feeling confused and sometimes disappointed for not accomplishing what I set out to do. Like so many other things in life, I failed to see something through until the end.

I found myself crawling back into my shell, in a world where I took little or no risks again. Taking one step at a time and not worrying too much about the future, worked for me, but this was an easier approach to justify when I believed I wouldn't be around much longer. Now, it just felt like I was being selfish.

This was the dilemma I found myself in. Maybe I needed to stop over thinking everything and accept the person I was right then. Maybe there was a way I could continue to live my life in the present and not worry about what was round the next corner. Who's to say this wasn't the best method to use anyway.

Spending several years caring for people, who have life debilitating illnesses, really puts things into perspective. It helps you to appreciate what you've got and how lucky you are.

Most of us can walk and talk. We can make choices and decisions for ourselves. These are things that we're all guilty of taking for granted.

One young lady I used to look after called Lucy had multiple disabilities. She had Cerebral Palsy and a severe curvature of the spine, leaving her with extremely limited movement. Moreover, she was an epileptic and had up to thirty seizures every day. Her skin was like tissue paper and she was prone to getting the most terrible pressure sores all over her body.

She couldn't communicate verbally, but it was obvious she was in considerable discomfort, as she spent much of each day crying. She would become even more upset if she needed to be moved or disturbed in anyway. Simple tasks like getting her dressed in a morning, turned into a major ordeal.

Inevitably, when staff discussed Lucy, the subject of euthanasia would be brought up, some would argue that she was suffering too greatly, and had little-to no quality of life. Due to her lack of communication, this was extremely difficult to ascertain, but I always argued strongly against this viewpoint.

Once a week we would take Lucy to a hydrotherapy pool. Once we got her supported in the warm water, she would lie there on her back contentedly smiling, whilst staring up at the sensory lights on the ceiling. She clearly loved this activity.

At the day centre she attended, there was an Olympic sized trampoline. We were able to hoist her on to it and with a great deal of support from staff, and extra cushioning for her protection, we were able to give her a gentle rocking sensation. This always resulted in a big smile and on rare occasions giggling!

It was wonderful to see her like that and most significantly; in my eyes it expelled the idea of her having no quality of life.

Life is very precious and providing someone's getting some pleasure out of it, however small, surely, it's worth continuing with. Coming back to me, I know this contradicts the fact that I tried to take my life, but at the time I wasn't getting any pleasure, I was in an extremely dark place. This may or may not justify what I planned to do. But for several weeks afterwards, I considered myself fortunate to still be around and I really wished I could have bottled these feelings up. But sadly, overtime they diminished. Even so, to this day I have to pinch myself that I'm still around, and it still feels like every day's a bonus.

TAKING THE ROUGH WITH THE SMOOTH

Even though, I was feeling more optimism than I had for some time, life was far from easy. Sadly, when you have clinical depression, it rarely is, even when you're having a positive spell, you find you have more bad days than good. It's all about how you manage these days and make the most of it when your illness loosens its grip.

On an average day, I feel like heavy weights have been strapped to my body, constantly tugging me down, like I'm struggling to keep my head above water. Contrary to what people keep telling me, I don't think I'm getting any better. If I am improving, it's happening far too slowly, I feel like I'm going to run out of time sooner rather than later.

My analogy is one of learning to drive. Let's say it takes you forty lessons to be confident enough to go in for your test. There's still no guarantee that you'll pass (Nerves can always take over on the day), but you at least have enough knowledge, and you know you're capable of doing whatever's asked of you. But what if your instructor speeds the whole process up and suddenly, you're expected to take your test after just four lessons. How would you feel then? You've only been on the main road once and barely even started on clutch control! You know the very basics and you're not even that confident with those! I know this is a silly example that would hopefully never happen, but it's also exactly how I feel with my illness. Sure, I am making some small improvements, such as being able to go short distances on my own and managing to help my mother with the weekly shop, but when it comes to the bigger picture I'm still petrified. I am nowhere near ready to drive the car on my own yet and I'm not sure I ever will be.

So, here's what I see happening, in the near future I see my benefits being taken off me, or I'll have to attend another medical, which will equate to the same thing, as I can't possibly put myself through one of those again. Even if I could, I'm liable to completely freeze, and fail to answer the questions properly.

I'll then have to watch as my bank account plummets, and I drift into bankruptcy.

I won't end up homeless, as my family won't allow this to happen, but I will end up being a massive burden on them, and I can't be that person, in fact I refuse to be that person.

As time goes by, I feel more and more useless and ashamed of the person I've become. If anything, I'm more fragile now than ever before. I feel totally inadequate when it comes to leading, what you'd call a normal life. Even though it seems like I'm gradually improving, I'm fed up with celebrating such small achievements.

Friends and family tell me how much they love me, irrespective of my illness and I believe them. In truth it's quite conceivable that they'll continue to support me, even if I never recover. The trouble is, I don't want people to have to put up with me. More to the point I'm not even sure I can put up with me for too much longer! It's sad to think that I hate myself but sometimes, it's difficult to find anything I do like.

It kills me when I see friends and family suffering and I'm unable to help them like I used to. They deserve a lot better from me, but sadly I can't see this ever happening.

In many respects I'm a child trapped in an adult's body, who's never dealt with the concept of growing up. Just like a child, my emotions are up and down like a seesaw; I can literally go from feelings of elation to ones of total despondency in a matter of minutes and when I do, it rarely makes any sense! Who is this imposter who's taken over my body? Maybe he was there all along but it's only now I'm letting him out.

Why have I become so fearful of life? Why am I so afraid of being an adult? On bad days I exhaust myself attempting to find an answer to these questions. Trying to navigate a path through my mind and somehow find a strategy to cope with everyday life, soon becomes implausible. I feel like I'm fighting a losing battle. I'm still unable to comprehend what makes me like I am, and that's extremely frustrating.

I crave a life with no complications. I'm aware this doesn't exist for anyone, but I can always dream.

Many of the people I used to look after, lacked the capacity to make important decisions for themselves. Their main concerns usually surrounded food and drink and routine toilet trips. I know I should be grateful for having all my faculties and this may sound selfish, but a big part of me envies the simplicity of their lives and wishes I had less to worry about in mine.

Have you ever had that dream with the sensation of falling? You're plummeting to the ground at a rapid speed and nothing's going to save you from the inevitable impact to come. Except you always wake up just before it happens. Most people would wake up with a massive sense of relief – thank god it was only a dream. I used to wake up frustrated that it was only a dream, both wishing and wondering how it would be in reality. How great it would be to go to sleep and never wake up. No more worries, no more confusions, no more fears, pressure, or expectations. No further disappointments, just a nice calm peace.

When you see someone crying, you immediately know something's wrong. Depending on what sort of person they are, they may need consoling, or they might prefer to be left alone, but either way at least you can tell they're upset. I'm upset too but I can't cry. On my bad days I feel overwhelming sadness, and this is compounded by the fact that I have no release. Wounded, down and out with a heavy weariness. Sometimes it's hard work just lifting my head off the pillow in a morning, some days I can't find a reason too. Even when I'm distressed and reach my absolute breaking point, I'm still unable to show my emotions. As the pressure builds, I get terrible headaches and sometimes a burning sensation behind my eyes, but never any tears! I can be desperate to sob my heart out, but still nothing!

I know it's not a physical abnormality, my eyes water like mad when I'm chopping onions. I just can't seem to cry at any other time. My close friends and family can tell when I'm struggling emotionally, but the rest of the world never sees what's behind my mask. I promised you that throughout this book I would try to be completely honest when sharing my feelings. If my statements ever contradict themselves, it's because my emotions generally fluctuate to such an extent. How I think and feel one day, can be totally different the next. I find this disturbing to say the least, but it's part of my depression and a sufferance I continue to endure. Even composing this book has consequences on my mental health. Seemingly, it's taking me forever, as some days, it's simply too painful to write.

Remember this has been me explaining my emotions on a bad day, thankfully it's not how I feel all the time. My doctor would say it's just my depression talking, or my negative persona taking over. When I'm able to do so, I try to remind myself that depression doesn't control me. I give myself a pep talk, trying to focus on the positive, of which there is plenty!

I say to myself: - 'stop *focusing on everything you're unable to do Shaun and try giving yourself a bit of credit for a change! You're still making a huge difference to people's lives. You're supporting your family, both physically and emotionally, despite feeling like crap most of the time! Your friends still love spending time with you and continue to seek your advice when they need it. Your teammates are always asking over you and wishing you well enough to come back to them. Your well-liked by so many people, and your making progress fighting this illness, so stop giving yourself such a hard time!*

When I think about fighting my illness, I'll never underestimate people power and I appreciate how fortunate I am, to have the support of such loving family and friends. People who continue to fight my corner, regardless of my extreme mood swings. Despite of these wonderful people, three things stand out as being life savers to me. Two of which I've already shared. The gentle breeze on the top of the quarry, which literally stopped me in my tracks, and the counselor, who miraculously got me talking, and even more miraculously had me ask for help! The third is a little different but equally significant. My table tennis was my saviour at high school and continues to be invaluable to this day. It's an essential form of escapism and something I couldn't currently live without.

FEAR OF FAILURE, FEAR OF SUCCESS

For as long as I can recall, I've always had an overwhelming fear of failure, and I'd go to great lengths to avoid standing out, as someone who can't do something.

During my first job working for the NHS, I had to undergo regular training in many different areas. The bosses would usually let me know in advance, the training subject and venue. If, for example they told me I was going to be attending a food hygiene course in two weeks' time. This would now become my obsession; I would spend every night on the Internet gathering as much information as humanly possible. Come the day, I would have swatted up so much, that I literally had enough knowledge to run the course myself!

I didn't do this in order to show off or to become any kind of teacher's pet, my intentions were quite the opposite. If I could get away with sitting quietly and saying nothing all day, that's precisely what I'd do, but if on the off chance, I was put on the spot I knew I'd have the answer and if they tried to shock us with a test, I should be able to comfortably breeze through it. This is how I like to approach any challenges in life. Excessive planning allows me to limit the number of surprises.

Of course, a life without surprises is unrealistic, however much effort you put into it. There'll always be times when you must deal with the unexpected, and this is where I've always fallen down.

During the same job, I was given the news that I had to attend a mystery team-building day. I'm ashamed to say I never made it and ended up having to phone in sick. I simply couldn't handle the thought of being unprepared. I found the whole thing terrifying and unachievable. Most people enjoy a bit of spontaneity, I can't imagine anything worse.

After a great deal of endeavor and countless application forms, I finally got myself a job outside of care. I remember feelings of relief to be entering a new sector. This could be exactly what I needed, a complete fresh start. Sadly, events didn't materialise this way, in fact, all it accomplished was me feeling even worse and incapable of doing anything right!

"You fucking simpleton! You complete imbecile! Claw grip, claw grip! Do you want to lose your fucking fingers!

Useless bastard! How brain dead are you! How long's it take to peel a fucking potato! Service! Service! Come on you fucking slow coach! What the fucks that? I'm not serving that crap! My grandkids could do a better job than that. Wrong fucking plate again Shaun, get a grip! Hopeless, hopeless, hopeless!"

These are just a sample of profanities directed at me, in my two weeks of hell working in a pub kitchen, by what I can only describe as a little Hitler of a landlady. Whilst there, I also had a baguette launched at my head because she didn't like the way I'd prepared it. I remember thinking, how long before she starts throwing knives at me! I found the screaming orders to be quite amusing, but the more I nervously smiled, the more her volume levels would increase.

On the way home from work one evening, I went to the late-night supermarket to buy various vegetables to practice on. You see, she liked them chopping to her exact specification. I would stay up to the early hours practicing, in a desperate attempt to avoid another scolding the following day. But inevitably, with her glaring over my shoulder, I continued to make mistakes and she continued her incessant ranting!

This job came shortly after getting attacked, in the care job, I wrote about earlier, a time when I was trying to come to terms with my panic attacks. So unfortunately, I already had major confidence issues and low self-esteem going into it. It was also my last job to date. After this, is when I went into the isolation and deep depression, I've already shared with you.

As well as being afraid of failure, it's fair to say I'm equally fearful of my success. Imagine for a minute you're back at school and two people are picking teams for a football match. Imagine you're the last to be picked. The reality is you've not been chosen by anyone, you're the excess baggage that nobody wants. This can be highly embarrassing and leave you feeling ostracised from the group.

In my eyes the only thing worse than this, is being chosen first, you're the schools star striker, everyone's relying on your genius to win the match and win all the inter school titles. All the attentions on you, there's no hiding place. You carry the team's burden of expectation on your shoulders.

I may have over dramatised this a bit, but it's close to how I felt at the time, playing in the table tennis league, being our teams' number one player and the guy expected to win all his matches. When you do occasionally lose a game, people make a huge deal out of it. The last season I managed to play before my illness forced me to take a sabbatical, I managed to remain unbeaten from September until February, a total of over forty matches. When I did lose it was put in the local newspaper with the headline 'Ellis Beaten! The article concentrated solely on the loss and mentioned nothing at all about my unbeaten run. It's this kind of unfair pressure, not to mention everything else going on in my life, that caused me to take a few years out from the game. In hindsight this was a mistake, as it turned out to be one of the few things that was keeping me going. But at the time it didn't seem this way, as my mental health demons were influencing everything in my life, causing me to dislike a game that I had loved for years.

Even presently, If I'm perfectly honest, there's a part of me, that's frightened by the thought of getting better and all the extra challenges it will bring. Not to mention people's expectations of me changing. When you're battling a long-term illness such as I am, it soon becomes a way of life. As much as I'm desperate to recover and lead what you'd call a normal life, this way of being is what I've got used to and most importantly it's what feels safe.

'We learn wisdom from failure much more than success. We often discover what we will do, by finding out what we will not' (Samuel Smiles)

'We haven't failed. We now know a thousand things that won't work, so we're that much closer to finding what will. I failed my way to success' (Thomas Edison)

MY BIG COMEBACK

When you're at your lowest ebb it's difficult to ever contemplate any kind of future. Just maneuvering through the day is challenging enough. But as you start to show signs of improvement, I think it's important to have goals, something positive to work towards. For me it was all about rejoining my teammates and playing competitive table tennis again. I knew that the actual playing of the sport wouldn't be a problem, as it's something I've enjoyed doing for several years (my comfort zone, you might say). Playing in the league involved either playing in a sports hall with lots of people present or alternatively playing in the back room of a pub or social club, a much more intimate and confined space, with only a handful of people. This would prove equally difficult, forcing me to be sociable and initiate small talk, something that's still hard work and unnerving. Even so, I found this an easier prospect and so choose a small venue for my first match back.

During the evening, I was only truly comfortable when it was my turn on the table, the problem being that most of the time you're sat watching. In these moments, I felt very self-conscious, like people were studying my every move, expecting me to have a major meltdown! Overall, though, things were going well, and I was coping much better than I'd expected. Halfway through the night I started feeling a bit claustrophobic, at this point I did the sensible thing and removed myself from the room. I just needed a five-minute breather and decided to go upstairs to the toilets. Once there I locked the door and sat myself on the throne. I was able to use mindfulness breathing techniques to calm myself and bring me back to the present. Pretty soon I was ready to rejoin the match, but then disaster struck! On attempting to leave the toilet, part of the lock broke off in my hand, leaving me trapped. I tried numerous methods to get myself out, but it was of no use, I wasn't going anywhere fast! Completely helpless until someone downstairs noticed my absence and came to my rescue. Twenty minutes later after all other options had been exhausted, my team-mates had to kick the door down.

Of all the times to get stuck in the loo it had to happen on my first game back! But it did happen, and remarkably the worst I felt was foolish. Shortly afterwards I was even able to laugh at my misfortune. Not long ago such an incident would have caused extreme panic in me, in fact I'm not sure I'd have survived it. Now I found my only concern was looking a bit silly.

Since that night, the more matches I played, the more relaxed I become. I now found myself halfway through the season and I couldn't remember what all the fuss was about. I was back loving the game again.

Sometime later, with league matches no longer posing a threat to me, I decided to step it up a level and enter a tournament. This would be a huge challenge, as it would involve being in a large sports hall with a high volume of people and having to remain in what would likely feel an intimidating environment for the entire day.

Inevitably the weeks running up to the event were filled with reoccurring nightmares and much trepidation. I couldn't believe I'd put myself in this position. It was crazy and idiotic of me to imagine I'd ever cope. I mean, let's just take a minute to absorb the facts: at this stage of my life, even though my health was improving, I still avoided groups at all costs. I hadn't been into the town centre for over two years; I avoided busy shops and any of the larger supermarkets. I went for walks at six in the morning for fear of running into people. I would strategically plan my day to avoid crowds. So, with all this in mind, how could I possibly face being in a room with over 500 people, all sucking in my air, nowhere for me to hide. What on earth was I thinking!

One thing I was able to do was rigorously plan the day. I had my best friend and my mother accompanying me. We were going the night before and stopping in a hotel, close by. All to avoid unnecessary rushing around on the day. We planned to get to the venue at least half an hour earlier, so I had time to acclimatise to my surroundings. Also, the room would gradually fill with people, rather than all at once, hopefully this would prove less daunting. Even though I was so well prepared, I still had no clue to how I would react on the day.

What I could never account for was what happened next. During our journey down whilst cruising at 70mph on the motorway, we had a blow out, two of our tyres literally ripped to shreds, causing us to violently swerve across the road. This was a terrifying experience to say the least, but miraculously no one was hurt. The car narrowly avoided colliding with a barrier or the cars that were in close proximity to us. My friend somehow managed to steer us onto the hard shoulder and we all breathed a huge sense of relief! We called the break down company and within an hour we were back on the road with two new tyres.

The weekend went ahead as planned but this incident helped me to put things into perspective, all the concerns I had, now seemed insignificant compared to what had just occurred. I felt grateful to still be here!

On the morning of the tournament, I was still very nervous, but by the time I'd played my first match and settled in, I found myself completely at ease and went on to have a great day. My first objective was simply to last the day in such a busy environment and that proved much easier than I could have imagined, in fact I was in my element competing again. For the first time in ages, I felt like I belonged somewhere. Significantly, I was able to forget about my illness for a while. I can't underestimate how huge an achievement that was for me, and it left me wondering what else I was capable of. It also left me feeling extremely optimistic for the future.

Even nowadays, table tennis feels like an alternative reality. A wonderful world, where I can relax and not feel out of my depth. My teammates understand about my anxiety and how different I am away from the sport. My opponents wouldn't recognize me in the real world, as I'm a shadow of the man they know. They would stare in disbelief, if they could see me constantly on edge, trying, and often failing to walk around the corner at the end of my street.

COMPETITIVE SPIRIT

I enjoy playing numerous sports and use each of them to escape from the pressures of everyday life. It's amazing how great it feels to smash a golf ball down the middle of the fairway or kick a football into the roof of the net. As well as the obvious benefits the exercise brings, sports can be an effective way to release tension. When playing table tennis in the league, the strength and camaraderie I get from being part of a team, is immeasurable. I really feel to be an important part of something. I'm trying to win, not just for myself, but for the other lads too. It helps me feel valued and significant, all of which increases my self-worth.

I've always been intrigued by the mentality of sports men and women. And how the great ones can raise their game against all kinds of adversity. My main sport is table tennis, and I've played in the local leagues now, for over 30 years. Way back in my past, I represented my county as a junior. I know some people might belittle this achievement cause it's only table tennis, but it takes a lot of hard work and dedication to reach that standard at any sport, and I felt immense pride every time I put my team shirt on. I'm still not a bad player, but in the grand scheme of things, I'm far from exceptional! I take the game less serious these days.

I suffer from anxiety and depression. Lately more and more people are talking about their mental health, including major sporting stars, who are in the public eye. I'm both amazed and inspired by these people, who have made it to the top of their sports, against all the odds. Believe me when I say, when depression takes its grip, it's hard enough to get yourself out of bed, have a wash and get dressed, let alone find the dedication needed to be a professional sports star. At it's worse, my depression has a major detrimental effect on my life, but if I can get out of the house and involve myself with exercise or any sporting activity, I instantly feel better. It's a far better medicine than any anti-depressant!

So, what turns a good sportsman into a great one? And can the same characteristics benefit you in everyday life, or maybe even help me battle my mental health? I was curious to ask other people what they thought. And so, I sent this survey out, to over a hundred people from various sporting backgrounds.

I've put together a list of some of the traits that are needed to be a great sports person. I did it with table tennis in mind, however the list should apply to any sport.

Please tick your top five, and number them 1-5 in order of importance (1 being the best)

- **Natural Ability**

- **Mentality/Self-belief-** An unwavering positivity, even when things are going Pete Tong!

- **Excel Under Pressure-** A good player can maintain their level for a crucial game point. An average player may fold under pressure. Only a great player can raise their game in these moments.

- **Tactical Nous-** A great understanding of how to play different styles of opponent and conditions.

- **Doggedness-** Never accept defeat!

- **Winning Ugly-** You can't always play your best, but great players find a way to win, irrespective of this.

- **Consistency-** Their performance level never seems to drop below 7 out of 10, even on a bad day.

- **Adaptability-** Able to resort to plan B or C when plan A's not working. Most of us mere mortals, think about what we should have done afterwards!

- **Reading of the Game- A** great player can pre-empt what their opponents going to do, and because of this, never seems rushed.

- **Single-minded Determination-** Win at all costs attitude, always seeking perfection, never truly satisfied with their performance.

The results of the survey were very interesting. Over a hundred people asked, and no two, chose the same answers. The top scorers were **Mentality/self-belief,** closely followed by **Natural ability. Single minded determination** and **Adaptability,** also scored highly, proving what I already thought, that much of what makes you great is found between the ears!

Of course, none of this is an exact science. I've got very little in the way of self-belief, but I'm still able to win a high percentage of my matches, despite not having the thing that's scored highest on my survey. Why is it then, that I'm an exception to the rule? The answer is simple. Table tennis is much more than just a sport to me. Sure, I have a competitive spirit, and sure, I love to win as much as anyone else does. But it's genuinely not the be all and end all. Years of battling my mental demons have helped me to put things, such as winning and losing, into perspective. This in turn, helps me to put far less pressure on myself. I've come to realise that success is much less important, than the way something makes you feel.

When my illness gets the better of me and prevents me from leaving the house, I'm fortunate enough to have great friends who offer me an abundance of reassurance and support. That being said, table tennis is the only activity where I feel relatively normal. At matches, I am Shaun- some guy who plays table tennis. I am not Shaun- some guy with an anxiety disorder.

Having an escape like this, is far more rewarding than any number of trophies or league titles I may accumulate. The feeling you get from being part of a team is invaluable. The support I've received from them, has helped me through two failed suicide attempts and continues to give me hope for the future. Perhaps having a good support network, should have also been included in my survey.

Top sports people can remain in the present and focus on one thing at once. They don't think about winning an event, or even who they're likely to meet in the next round. All they focus on is winning the next point or how they're going to play the next shot.

This is a great mentality to have and one you can take into other aspects of life, when undertaking any given task. Last week my friend and I started doing some gardening work for an elderly neighbour. At first glance, we were both shocked by what we saw, the task appeared overwhelming and even insurmountable. we couldn't believe what we'd let ourselves in for! The area between two garages had clearly been used as a dumping ground for rubbish, and judging by the amount, this had been going on for a long time. We'd have to clear all this before we even got to the garden. To say it was overgrown was a massive understatement, in fact the jungle that confronted us was inexplicable. Instead of freaking out, which would have been very easy, we broke the task down into manageable segments. Before we knew it, we'd cleared the rubbish and was making a start on the garden. We haven't finished yet, but by taking it one small step at a time, it won't be long before we've achieved what first appeared to be an impossible job.

Back to the survey, the discrepancies from the results show, that most of us, probably don't know exactly what makes you great. Our perceptions on greatness also vary. Is the sportsman who wins his matches every week, the great one? Or could it be his opponent, who rarely wins, but never lets his head go down, and always supports his team despite how his own games are going? Is it the shrewd businessman who makes millions on a single deal? Or should we be more impressed by the single mother, having to work two jobs to provide for her kids, completely selfless and willing to go short of things for the sake of her family.

People with depression often push others away, I did this for a long time. The reason being, I didn't feel worthy of the support and didn't want to impose my current self onto people who I cared for. I was also very confused and struggling to get my head around things, so how could I possibly expect anyone else to understand? Including others, felt like too much of an effort, I was already exhausted and at an all-time low. Why would I ever inflict this onto somebody else. You end up feeling unworthy of the help and they feel hopeless for not being able to provide it! You believe that accepting the help is putting an unnecessary burden on them, but for them not being able to help is much more damaging. Whilst I felt this way, I didn't play table tennis in the league for two years.

Opening up was far from easy, but every time I did, I felt a huge sense of relief, I was left pleasantly surprised by people's reactions. It's easy to pre-empt how you think others view you, but your presumptions are often completely wrong. Having the support of my teammates has given me extra strength to fight my depression. My only regret is that I kept it from them, for as long as I did. Mental health is nothing to be ashamed of, and I wish that more people would share their stories.

Believe it or not, I wouldn't describe myself as a competitive person, the majority of games and sports I take part in, I couldn't care less whether I win or lose, as long as I don't stand out as being really bad!

Table Tennis is the exception to this rule. Right from the first time I picked a bat up, as a six-year-old at a Butlins holiday camp. I've become addicted and devoted to being the best I can. Why this sport, as opposed to others? Well for starters, I found the game excruciating, why wasn't the ball going where I wanted it to? Why couldn't I keep it on the table for more than two shots? Why was my brother so much better than me? For the remainder of our holiday stay I played every day in an attempt to improve, and my parents had to endure a number of strops from me along the way. By the end of the week, I was completely hooked.

My dad did some fishing around and found a local youth club that was doing a beginner's class on a Monday night. He took me along, I loved it, and I've never looked back since.

I wouldn't describe myself as the most naturally gifted of players. I never have been, but somehow with hard work and determination, as a junior player (Under 17) I reached the highest ranking of number two in Yorkshire and number ten in the country. Even at senior level I have won plenty, and I'm still classed as one of the best in my local area. I put all this down to being highly competitive at the sport and hating to lose. Any weaknesses I had I would soon turn into strengths, by labourish training, I would not stop practicing a certain shot until I got it right and could virtually do it in my sleep! What I lacked in ability, I made up for with tactical nous. Over the years I have defeated many better players than myself, purely due to having a better strategy than them.

As a kid, when my dad was taking me round the tournament circuit, I had a little book that I wrote my tactics in. especially if I lost to an opponent, I would write their name down and what it was about their game that I struggled with. Then I'd take it back to my coach and we would use it as a good incentive to keep me improving. He'd give me set exercise programs, which I'd follow relentlessly; to avoid making the same mistakes in future matches. To get to a decent standard at any sport takes copious amounts of self-discipline and endurance.

These days I don't take it half as seriously, but one thing that's always remained the same, is my hatred of losing, I still do everything in my power to avoid this from happening.

As I've touched upon earlier in the book, I get on extremely well with my teammates and people from the opposing teams, but when I'm at the table, I become very single minded and determined to beat whoever's in front of me. There's plenty of time for pleasantries later in the pub! When I'm up against a formidable opponent, I double my efforts and tend to relish the challenge.

So why can't I adopt this same approach to other challenges in my life, such as dealing with my depression and moving on in the future.

I need to view every obstacle I come up against, as a new opponent, and just like with an opponent; I can weigh it up and adopt the right strategy to beat it.

Obviously, I have more confidence in myself when it comes to Table Tennis, because I know it's something, I'm good at. As I've explained though, this hasn't always been the case, it's took hard work to achieve what I have from the game. Surely with all my competitive qualities, including my hard work and determination, my passion and drive and learning from my mistakes. Not to mention my discipline. Surely, I can condition my body and mind to overcome anything. If I can keep the same positive ethos, I might just surprise myself.

'If we did all the things, we are capable of doing we would truly astound ourselves' (Thomas Edison)

In sports, I'm somehow able to aim higher and push myself further. I manage to find that extra grit and determination to be the best that I can be. To do this, I aim for perfection and I'm rarely satisfied by the standards I achieve. I wish I could bottle some of this single mindedness up in other aspects of life. It's highly frustrating to say the least, but instead of doing this, when I come up against a challenge or task, I end up aiming much lower. Whereas in sports I'm wanting as

113

close to perfection as I can get, for everything else I'm happy with being mediocre at best. I often talk myself into failing before I've even begun, and that's if I begin at all! An overriding fear of being the worst, of looking like a complete fool and being ridiculed by everyone, normally prevents me from trying anything new. It leads to an unhealthy avoidance, of even the simplest of tasks. Ultimately it leads to the person I am now, a person who takes few risks in life. Whose confidence and self-esteem has been depleted and desperately needs building back up.

Fortunately for me, I have a lot of good people around to help me to do this.

There's been times in the past when I've tried and failed miserably at tasks. In doing so I've become a laughingstock, but this is the same for most people, let's face it nobody's perfect. In truth these occurrences, have been few and far between but when they have happened, I've been left feeling extremely small, as I'm transported back to being a little boy cowering in a corner, with all the school bullies pointing and sniggering.

Naturally, this is a scary place to be and not one that I want to revisit too often.

But on the other hand, I know that if I don't try things, I'm not going to have any new experiences, the very same experiences that make life worth living.

I need to remind myself that I'm an adult now and most people I encounter will not be as cruel as the bullies. One or two maybe, but certainly not enough to prevent me from living my life.

ADDICTION

Time for a quick recap.

I've already shared with you, many of the significant events in my life, certainly the ones pertaining to my mental health. From way back at high school being a frightened little boy, leading closer to present day were in some respects, I'm still that same frightened little boy, I hope I've given you an insight into the rollercoaster of emotions I've endured along the way.

I was now 38, just 18 months prior to writing this book. I still had my carer visiting once a week, and on occasions with his help, I was able to leave the house independently. Admittedly, I wasn't going far, on a good day I could get to the corner shop and back. But this was still a huge step forward, and after spending a prolonged period trapped in the house, it was an amazing relief to get some fresh air, without having to rely on other people's availability.

My table tennis was also going well, I was frequently playing in the league now, and loving the game again. It still felt a bit surreal at times (like being in another world), but I recognised how it was benefiting me, and it genuinely gave me something to look forward to every week.

My progress, although painfully slow, was certainly moving in the right direction. I wasn't able to work, but kept myself busy writing small articles for magazines, this in turn, led to me creating my own mental health blog. Every time I received positive feedback, it gave me a boost, but more significantly, I was able to help people with similar issues to me, which of course, gave me a great sense of purpose.

Throughout my life, it's been like I'm climbing a steep precipice, with an invisible elastic band strapped around my waist. Each time I'm close to eyeing anything resembling the top, the band tightens, slowing my progress, until inevitably it twangs, and I'm sent hurtling back down to earth. I dust myself off and try again, but this is becoming increasingly difficult to do. I am fast running out of the resilience I need to keep climbing! At this stage of my story, things were going too well, I was beginning to feel hope, a sensation that had remained alien for a long time. But then, just as the fog was parting,

TWANG.........!

AN ADDICT'S STORY

Just one more spin of the wheel

Just one more turn of the card
Five more minutes and I'll stop, I swear!
Win or lose, this is the last 50 quid for the day
I know what I said but …...
I have this under control, honestly!
Once I'm in the bonus game, I promise I'll stop.
I know what I said but ……

I've always liked a flutter. When I was younger whilst on nights out with the lads, it's fair to say, I spent too much on the bandits, but it was always money I could afford to lose. I enjoyed an occasional sporting bet as well, but due to my anxiety, and there being no bookies close to home, I hadn't been able to do this for several years. That is until 18months ago, when I discovered online gambling. I got home late from a table tennis match one evening, I was already feeling a bit down, as I'd not had the best of nights, and in my head, I'd cost the team a victory. I was watching television and unwinding before bed, when I saw an advertisement for a gaming company. It was easy to register, and so I thought why not? This could be just the thing to cheer me up. On this occasion it had the desired effect, but soon after, led to endless complications. Complications that led to me attempting suicide for a second time.

We all have our vices, and sadly mine is gambling. It pains me to admit it, but I am in fact, an addict, and my addiction torments me every day. It's cost me my entire life savings, not to mention the trust of my family and friends. I'm horrified when I think back. Something that was once just a bit of fun, a small bet once in a blue moon. How can that have escalated into being such a serious problem?

I believe that gambling companies, in general, prey on the vulnerable, and as someone who has spent years battling with clinical depression, I fall into that category. As I've shared with you, my anxiety can prevent me from leaving the house, often for long periods of time. I soon become isolated and need someone or something to turn to. In these difficult moments, the only communication I have with the outside world, comes from the gaming sites. Scores of text messages, relentless in their nature. Urging me to come back to their site, claiming that they have missed me. Promising me the best deals I can imagine. Offering me free spins as an incentive, on games which they claim to have a 97% winning guarantee. What they fail to tell you, is the scale of the winnings in comparison to the amount you've staked. To put it simply, you might win 20 pence, but it's cost you £2.50 for the spin in the first place, so the reality is you've lost

£2.30! I'd like to think I'm not a complete fool! Deep down I know these companies couldn't care less about me. But when I'm in a desperate state, all rational thought seems to desert me. I'm left clinging to whatever glimmer of hope there is.

I become engrossed in the games, **CLICK, CLICK, CLICK.** Every click equates to one more spin of the reels, costing me two pounds a time (sometimes more). I remember one night, winning 200 quid on a single spin but not being satisfied by this, (my obsession with getting into the bonus feature game exceeded any kind of logic), I quickly blew the 200 I'd won, plus another 500 on top! I completely lost track of time as I become fixated with the game. It's often 6 o clock in the morning before I go to bed. During this time, I drink copious amounts of alcohol, it seems one addiction fuels another. The following day I stare at my bank balance in disbelief, when I discover how much money I've blown, at best I feel physically sick - at worst I feel suicidal. These painful shocks have had little effect though. Even now If I had the means to gamble, I would continue to do so. You could call it utter stupidity, but I still have this wild optimism that my luck must change at some point. *I mean it must, mustn't it?* Even on the rare occasions it has, and I've had a few wins, I've convinced myself that I'm now on a winning streak! This results in me playing with higher stakes and losing even more money. There's only ever one winner in this process and it's never going to be me. The saying **QUIT WHILST YOU'RE AHEAD** is clearly not one that is in my vocabulary! I'm deeply ashamed when I think of all the money I've lost and what could have been if I'd stopped sooner. Just to help you realise the scale of my loses, on one fatal night, I blew eight and a half thousand pounds, in 20 minutes of madness, on a roulette wheel. In no time at all, I'd flushed my entire life savings down the toilet! The frightening thing is, if I'd had more money in the bank, I wouldn't have hesitated to continue betting, but as it is, I'd spent my overdraft limit and the bank wouldn't allow me to. Words could never describe the shame and misery I felt in this moment. How could I ever face my family after this? I thought about how long it had taken, to get my bank account looking as healthy as it was. How many years of putting a little aside? And then how long It had taken to blow the entire lot! What I desperately wanted, was to go to sleep and never wake up. I attempted to accomplish this fete by taking a cocktail of pills, including a full pack of antidepressants and several paracetamols, washed down with half a bottle of whisky. I expected this to be my final cowardly act. Instead, the next day I woke up covered in vomit and feeling as sick as I'd ever felt, x10! I was violently sick, off and on for the rest of the day, and unable to stomach anything proper for days afterwards. In truth, I probably should have been admitted into hospital, but I remember how my first suicide attempt had affected my family and I wasn't ready to tell them what I'd done, or why I'd done it.

The temptation to gamble is always going to be there, but I have now put things in place to make it as difficult as possible. For starters I've cancelled all my existing gaming accounts and given my debit cards to my family to take charge of on a temporary basis (or however long it takes). Like I say, the nearest bookies are too far to get to on my own, due to my anxiety issues. So, it's pretty much impossible for me to gamble. None of these precautions can make up for the money I've lost, but they will hopefully prevent me from getting into more hot water in the future. It's so hard somedays, as I continue to get the urges to play my favorite slots. What's happened should be enough to deter me from ever wanting to play again, but to be honest it doesn't. I really miss the buzz I get, the excitement of the big money bet. I've never been able to replicate this feeling (although winning table tennis tournaments comes close), it's almost like a drug!

I sympathise with anyone experiencing an unhealthy addiction and understand that will-power alone doesn't always solve the problem, however strong minded you think you are. I have now accepted that once again I need extra support and hope that my story inspires others to do the same.

So here I am now, present day. All tablets in the house are locked in a safe, and I receive my prescriptions weekly, instead of monthly, for my own protection. My mother's still in charge of my cash card, I have no idea where she keeps it, and I have to ask permission to use it. The sad reality is, that as a gambling addict, no matter how many restrictions you put in place, if we really want to, we will find a way to gamble. Addicts go to great lengths to fuel their addictions. In total I cancelled over 30 gaming sites and went several months cold turkey as they say! But crucially, I forgot one. They left me alone for a while, but when I received the inevitable email with the tempting offer of free spins, it was too much to resist. I was soon to become dangerously engrossed in the game again. Just like that, I was back to square one, revisiting my overdraft and chasing my loses. There's no excuse for what I did, and believe me I feel deeply ashamed, but It's not as simple as just wanting to gamble, it's a need or deep desire that takes over everything. Dishonesty and deceitfulness become a way of life. I'm sad to say, I've lied to my family on numerous occasions. I've borrowed money from friends and blown it the following day. Eventually I had to come clean to my mother, who has now bailed me out yet again! So, I guess it's not the rosiest end to my story, I appologise for this, but that being said I'm still here, and that's got to count for something! I'm only 40, and so, it's far from the end for me. Writing this book continues to give me a purpose and welcome distraction, as every day I persist in the battle against my mental demons.

PART TWO
SELF-HELP/ADVICE

In this section I share many of the coping strategies that continue to help me manage my illness. I am not a medical expert; however, I have worked in the mental health sector and experienced the symptoms of anxiety and depression for several years now. I appreciate that everyone is different, what works for one person may not work for another. The information I give should only be taken as advice given from one sufferer to another. Much of what I share pertains to your psychological wellbeing, therefore can be useful to anyone, even those who don't have a mental health disorder.

ESCAPE TO A NICER REALITY

Sat on a bench at the far side of the park, far away from the noise of the children's play area; I'm enjoying the stillness surrounding me. What can I see? A perfect blue sky with the occasional white cotton cloud. If I look closely, I can make out different shapes in the clouds, it's fun to do so. This one looks just like a dog jumping for its ball. Golden leaves are beginning to form on the trees. Birds are tweeting their afternoon songs. Butterflies are flying side by side on the delicate breeze, performing a hypnotic dance just for me. A fluffy dandelion seed floats up inches away from my face and disappears into the distance.

I shut my eyes and feel the warm autumn sunshine against my forehead. I'm concentrating on slowing down now and relaxing. Starting with my breathing, I take deep breaths in through my nose and out through my mouth, I allow myself to be consumed by the serene beauty all around me. I can feel myself shutting down, leaving all my troubles behind me, and being one with nature, nothing to prove, no expectations, just a perfect moment. It's ok to feel small in its presence, and I do feel small in this tranquil solitude.

I have a few special places I like to visit, which I call my thinking spots. Although I guess they shouldn't be called this, as I go solely with the intention of switching off and escaping from the day-to-day pressures of life.

The places I choose tend to be out of the way, often high up on a hill, where there are few people around, and I have the benefit of some stunning views. Your special place could be totally different to mine; a lot of people find sitting by a riverbank and listening to flowing water, a calming experience. Unfortunately, all this does for me is makes me desperate for the loo! The important thing is, you view the place as an escape, or a nicer reality.

So anywhere that you can sit peacefully and be mindful of your surroundings, will do fine. Allow yourself to take notice of every little moment, almost as if the world and time has gone into slow motion and you're suddenly aware of everything around you. Every detail from the humming insects scurrying on the ground, to the individual leaves rustling in the trees. All the small things that you wouldn't usually notice when you're rushing your way through life. If you're struggling to switch off your busy mind, don't worry, we all have trouble doing this. Try starting with your breathing. As you breathe deep breaths in through your nose and out through your mouth, concentrate on this sensation. Notice how your chest is rhythmically rising and falling. Try slowing everything down. Try living in this moment for a while, it's the only thing that matters right now. You deserve this time to yourself. Gradually as you become more relaxed, you'll become acutely aware of all the minute things happening around you. Allow your senses to take over. What can you feel? What can you hear? I say, take time to see the beauty of the world; it's far too easy to take it for granted.

Happiness is a butterfly which, when pursued, is always beyond our grasp, but which, if you sit down quietly, may alight upon you (Nathaniel Hawthorne)

Time moves quickly and that's why it's important not to waste a single moment. All the small day to day experiences are much more significant than you think. Most of us rush from one task to the next and all the simple pleasures end up passing us by.

A friend asked me a good question the other day. He asked 'If someone told you that you only had a week to live, what would you want to do in terms of enjoyment? Here is what I came up with:

- Obviously, I'd want to spend quality time with my family and friends.
- Maybe a countryside walk with my brother.
- A milkshake with my friend in our favourite café.
- A couple of ice-cold beers in my best mate's garden.
- A picnic with my mum at our favourite lake.
- One last game of table tennis with my teammates.
- One last round of golf at my favourite course.
- Watching a classic film, like Goodfellas, whilst indulging in some Ben and Jerry's ice cream.

Hang on a minute, I did all this last week (all except the round of golf) and I'm still here! You might question why I haven't got anything more elaborate on my list, but would you really want to cram as many things in as you can, or like me, would you prefer to keep it simple and stick to what makes you happy?

I am a suicide survivor.

When I planned to kill myself, rather than just a week, I gave myself a full month to savour my last moments. Once I'd sorted all the practical stuff, like making sure my debts were all paid off and that I left my family enough money aside for the funeral. Once I'd sorted all this, all that was left to do, was to keep things simple and enjoy the time I had left. This was not a solemn time, it turned out to be a great time and a very honest one, I no longer had to pretend to be something I'm not. I found I could reflect on all the positive and completely live in the moment. No more worries about the future, what future, Ha!

More than just a feeling of relief, all my senses were suddenly heightened. I remember thinking, this might be the last time I see this, So I'm going to make sure I really see it! This could be the last time I feel this, so I'm going to truly feel it! I was noticing and appreciating more than I ever had before.

Have you ever quit a job which you really hated? you hand your resignation letter in and straight away it feels like a huge weight has been lifted. Whilst you're working your notice period, suddenly, things don't seem so bad, you might even start to wonder whether you've made the right decision to leave. I'd decided to make the ultimate quit, quitting on life, and all though I still thought I'd made the right decision, I was far from certain.

Time is a precious commodity, especially in these difficult times, when were all feeling the effects of the Corona virus pandemic. Even whilst in lockdown there are still places you can find to escape for some much needed me time. I'm currently sat in my garden, in my favourite spot. Why is it my favourite spot? Because it's secluded and I feel safe, not a single sole in sight. I'm not entirely alone though, Birds are tweeting their evening songs and an occasional bumblebee is buzzing past, all far too preoccupied to acknowledge my existence. I look up to see a never-ending blanket of blue and the sun setting in the distance, creating a pinkish purplish haze across the horizon. Some evenings this can create a kaleidoscope of colours, and what with the birds performing their bedtime symphony, it truly is a masterpiece of a scene! I have finished my daily meditations now and I'm truly alone with just my own thoughts for company. Not always great for a depressant I know, but right now it feels perfect.

And what does an intelligent budding writer think about in these moments of bliss? Well, you'll be surprised to hear, nothing too deep and meaningful! Believe it or not, right now, I'm thinking about time spent sat on the toilet! Weird I know, but please bear with me. let us just say, for arguments sake, that the average person spends 10 minutes a day sat on the throne, and let's just say that that person lives until there 80 years old. That equates to 291200 minutes in a lifetime, or 4853 hours, or approximately 202 days! What a huge waste of time and effort! Why can't we be like horses who do their business whilst on the move! Granted it can't really be helped, it's the way things have to be. However, it's got me thinking about how much time we do waste, time that we could do something about. How many of us are simply going through the motions, rushing from one event to the next and completely missing the whole point? The point being that life's about the experience. It's not just what you can reach out and touch, it's how these things make you feel that truly counts. How many people continue to let life pass them by?

Perhaps because of my experiences, my eyes have been opened wider than most, and perhaps I've learnt to take less for granted. Nobody, apart from me can appreciate how close I came that near fatal day at the top of the quarry, but thankfully, for whatever reason, I had a last second change of heart. I've discovered over time, that suicide is nothing to be ashamed of, and in fact being able to talk openly about it really helps me. I also understand that not everyone Is like me and for some, revisiting that moment of their lives is far too painful.

In the few weeks that proceeded my attempt, I saw more and felt more than I had in an entire lifetime. I know that must sound a bit farfetched, but it's true. For all intents and purposes, I shouldn't have been here anymore. It therefore felt like I'd been given a second chance. even now it sometimes feels like I'm living on bonus time. If I could have found a way to bottle up these emotions, I would have done so, but obviously over time they faded, it's unrealistic to think you can stay on cloud nine indefinitely!

I now find happiness in the strangest of places, like sat right here on this garden swing. This refreshingly cool breeze has probably always been there, but I've never allowed myself the time to truly feel it. Practicing mindfulness allows me to notice and appreciate all the finer details. It helps me to put things in perspective and worry less about the future. With my anxiety issues, these meditation techniques have become a vital coping tool, but even if I didn't have a mental health illness, I would still recommend them. Everyone has stressful moments, times when they're guilty of overcomplicating things. Mindfulness can help bring you back to the present and remind you that the only thing you can control, is the here and now. Not everyone is fortunate to have a nice garden to practice their mindfulness, not to mention the unpredictable nature of our British weather. Now, I for one like the rain (probably because there's not as many folks around and possibly because I'm slightly odd!) but I appreciate that not everyone does. Therefore, it's a good idea to have a few spots in your memory bank. One of my favourites is in Jamaica, a place I've been fortunate to visit twice in my lifetime, but somewhere I can easily go back too, just by being in a quiet room and closing my eyes.

I imagine myself sat on a wall outside my beech hut, looking out to sea. It's the end of the evening and I'm having a rum and coke before I retire to bed. Just below me on the beach, dozens of baby crabs are burrowing holes in the sand and then popping their heads up somewhere else. Like a big game of hide and seek, it's fascinating to watch them at play.

Looking out to the stillness of the sea, a cruise ship appears as a small dot on the horizon. A distant lightning storm lights up the whole scene creating an incredible spectacle. Breath-taking and beautiful, like my own miniature paradise. I remember never wanting to leave this perfect moment.

All these places-the ones in my memory, and the ones I'm able to visit regular, all help remind me that life's not that bad. I use them to de-stress and put my problems into perspective, or sometimes simply as a method of cheering myself up when I'm having a down day. However busy and hectic your life gets; I recommend that you find some time to **escape to a nicer reality.**

10 TIPS ON MANAGING YOUR ANXIETY

Here are my 10 simple steps to help manage your **anxiety** and still live a fulfilled life.

1/ REPETITION

We've all come across those annoying people who seem to be good at everything they turn their hand to! Of course, most of us are not like this, and the first time we try something new can be difficult. When you are unsure or not confident in what you're doing, you're kind of learning as you go. For someone with anxiety, the self-doubt in us massively increases, often making the task seem insurmountable, as we put far too much emphasis on what could go wrong. Even simple tasks that we've previously accomplished stress free, suddenly become very daunting. For those of you who don't suffer with excess anxiety, I would best describe it as learning to walk again. I'm talking about things like going to the shops, having a meal out, visiting a friend or even talking to the neighbours! all these things are difficult for us, but all become less challenging the more we do them. By repeating an activity regularly enough, difficult soon turns into manageable, manageable turns into easy and before you know it, you're wondering why you were worrying so much in the first place!

2/ PLANNING

Presently due to my anxiety, I have to plan a great deal. Some might call it excessive, but I call it necessary, and the best way for me to function in life. It helps me, to detail every stage of a journey or task.

- When will be the quietest time to visit somewhere?
- Can I familiarise myself with an environment to limit the number of surprises I may encounter? Where possible I try to do a recce of the area beforehand.
- Knowing where all the nearest exits are in a building. Psychologically, this helps me feel less enclosed and limits the chances of me having a panic attack. If the situation arises and my stress levels become too much, knowing I have a quick way to get home is also a big reassurance.
- Knowing what you can achieve on the day. It's important to continue to push yourself but at the same time you need to accept that you have an illness, and you'll have good days and bad. It's equally important therefore, not to beat

yourself up, if you don't achieve what you've initially set out to do.

I imagine you're probably sick of being told to take small manageable steps, but it's the best advice!

3/ TRICKING YOUR MIND

Often, it's the enormity of a task that can lead to excessive anxiety. What you can do to counteract this, is to split what you must do into manageable segments. Once you have completed stage 1 you can move onto stage 2, all the time only concentrating on the part you are doing, never looking too far ahead and risking causing yourself unnecessary stress. This is something that I would recommend to anyone, irrespective of if you have a mental health illness or not. It's also something that's easier said than done, I appreciate this, but maybe using some of the breathing exercises I shared in the last chapter, might help you remain in the present, so you're able to give it a go.

4/ BREATHING YOUR WAY TO CALM

Taking some deep breaths in through your nose before exhaling slowly through your mouth and watching the steady rise and fall of your chest, is one of the best proven methods for calming your anxiety. There's probably a very good technical reason for this, something along the lines of sending messages to that part of your brain which trigger a relaxation response in your body. What I do know, is that it helps slow your heart rate down. It helps release physical tension in your body, and importantly it gives you something else to focus your mind on, which can only be beneficial to your mental well-being.

5/ CIRCULAR JOURNEYS

Imagine doing a 4-mile walk. You walk 2 miles to a certain point and then turn around and walk the same route back.

Now imagine you do a walk the exact same distance, but instead of reaching a certain point and then turning around, you do a full circle. You still end up back where you started, but it somehow feels much shorter, and for me, much less stressful. This is clearly just a trick of the mind as you are going the exact same distance, but what you can do, is convince yourself that you're always on your way back home. I for one find this much more reassuring. An equally effective method is to have someone drop you off at your destination and then walk home. Again, there's something comforting about always being on your way back home.

6/ DISTRACTIONS

Music is a great distraction when you're feeling anxious. listening to favourite tunes can be very relaxing, help you to unwind and forget about the pressures of life. Some people choose to download meditations or mindfulness breathing exercises. When I'm out and about on my own I'm often very anxious. I feel extremely vulnerable, like everyone's a potential threat. It's in these moments that I desperately need something else to focus my mind. I find simple methods work best, such as tapping the tips of my fingers together, counting my steps or repeating a positive mantra in my head. If this fails to distract me, I phone a friend. Sometimes It's a good idea to warn them before hand to make sure they're going to be available!

7/ REASSURANCES

My family and friends provide me with amazing support. They are there for me when I'm having a bad day and I'm self-doubting myself. They remind me of all that I'm doing well and encourage me to keep going. When I'm having a good day and managing to achieve my goals, they're there to celebrate with me. If I'm attempting to go somewhere independently, it's always reassuring to know I have a family member on hand to come and rescue me if the situation arises. I appreciate that not everyone has this support and that I'm very fortunate, but there are other methods you can use to help alleviate your anxiety.

Having a positive mantra, you repeat when you're feeling stressed works well for some people.

Some people need something more substantial than this. I have written reminders for different situations. I simply read through these before leaving the house and they act as a great positive reinforcement. Pictures of achievements can have the same effect. Anything that embraces the strong person you are, someone who is in control of their emotions, and will achieve whatever they set out to do.

8/ PERSPECTIVE

For anxious people it's so easy to blow things out of all proportion, believe me I'm a world leader at this! You can see obstacles that simply don't exist. In these moments it's important to take some deep breaths and try to focus on the here and now. Remember, most of what you're experiencing is completely irrational and in reality, you're in total control of your own destiny. By taking your time and dealing with one thing at a time, you'll soon see that the task in hand is far less intimidating than you first imagined it to be. In life, danger is real and will always exist, but fear is just a state of mind. Try to face up to your fears. Putting things into perspective is something that's vital for managing your mental health. I'll elaborate more on this later in the book.

9/ EXERCISE/PHYSICAL LABOUR

The mind will always function better if you look after your physical body. If you're feeling low or anxious, you may become lethargic and unmotivated. As you feel compelled to be less active, you can soon get caught up in a harmful cycle. It's hard, I know, but this is the time you need to do something. Exercise can stimulate the parts of the brain that improve mood. You are more likely to feel good about yourself, as it can give you a sense of achievement. I also find exercise to be a great therapy and a way to escape from the pressures of life. It can help with concentration and focus, and importantly allow you to take back some control.

10/ DON'T VIEW IT AS YOUR ENEMY

You mustn't always view anxiety as your enemy. It could also be described as the cautious part of your persona, and It can be extremely helpful in keeping you safe. If the cave man weren't anxious about the approaching dinosaur, he wouldn't last very long! Nervous energy can lead to an adrenaline rush. Top athletes and pop stars can use this as a way to enhance their performance. The secret is learning to control it and not letting it take over and control you.

The tips I have given in this chapter, are simply things that have worked best for me. Neither should they be viewed as a magic cure, I'm afraid there is no quick fix when it comes to mental health. I am not an expert in the field but do have first-hand experience of living with anxiety and depression. These are simply some of the techniques that have helped me to manage my illness.

COPING TOOLS

A coping tool can be anything that helps you deal with your anxiety and depression. Anything that makes life a little easier. It could work as a distraction technique or be of therapeutic value to you.

I find reading a fictional book to be helpful; I can soon get lost in an imaginary story line and forget all about my own issues in the real world. A good film or favourite television program can have the same effect. For the more technically minded, podcasts can provide hours of interest on a wide range of subjects.

I am finding writing this book to be particularly useful too. As well as helping me to work through my illness and understand it better, it's also given me a purpose and is keeping my mind occupied, which is essential for someone with depression. Writing can be a valuable alternative for those not ready to talk about their issues, by simply taking a blank piece of paper and freewriting whatever comes to mind. Try to write continuously during this time. It doesn't have to make any sense, you don't even have to form sentences, random words will do just fine. I used to write some very dark material using this technique. Some, or all might be negative, but that doesn't matter, as once you've finished you can screw it up, roll it in a ball and throw it in the bin. I hope you'll find this to be a cathartic outlet, as I did.

I like to keep myself fit and any type of exercise can also be used as a great coping tool. It's a well-known fact that when you take part in physical fitness, chemicals are released in your brain that make you feel good and therefore will help to boost your self-esteem. Hence the saying healthy body, healthy mind. It can also give you a goal to work towards. For example, I got myself a Fit Bit, which amongst other things, measures how many steps you take when you're out and about. It's fun to try and beat your record from the previous week and might give you more of an incentive to leave the house. 2500 steps equates to 1 mile, which means if you do approximately 66,500 steps you have completed a full marathon!

It's always been important for me to feel in control. Exercise helps me to take control back of my body and this in turn can give me the confidence to start taking charge of other situations in my life. Walking in the countryside and the peacefulness that comes with this is a great aid for switching off, completely unwinding and being one with nature. There is no better therapy than this for me.

As I've already alluded to, I enjoy playing numerous sports and I use each of them as a way to escape from the everyday pressures of life, and an effective way of releasing tension. Being part of a team helps me feel valued and significant, all of which increases my self-worth.

Professional therapists can also play a significant role (I appreciate it's not for everyone). They have helped me with breathing techniques, meditation, mindfulness, and the use of pressure points. All of which can be used to relieve stress and, in my case, prevent me from having a full-blown panic attack. Anything that might stop this from occurring, has got to be worth a try.

In counselling I had a time and place to go every week, where I was encouraged to share my emotions in an environment where I could be totally open and honest, without running the risk of upsetting anyone. At the end of each session, I tried to leave any negative energy behind me in the room, so I could start a fresh.

It's not always easy to talk about your feelings, in fact at times it can be really exhausting and involve visiting some uncomfortable places. As hard as it can be, I always feel the benefit afterwards, when it feels like a huge weight has been lifted.

Just like my medication, my counselling was a necessary tool in my life at that time.

Something else I would struggle to do without are my amazing friends and family. The majority are aware of my illness and its effects, but still choose to help me through it. They can be a welcome distraction when I'm feeling low and need cheering up. They are a great support to me and understand that due to my anxiety, sometimes plans need to change. They never get frustrated however often this happens.

'A real friend is one that walks in when the rest of the world walks out' (Walter Winchell- American journalist)

I have a scrapbook that I'm constantly adding photos too, both past and present. This is one of the best instruments I have for dealing with my depression. Showing special memories of time spent with friends and family, favourite places I have visited and moments I'm proud of, has the desired effect of brightening up my day.

As well as this I also have a book of little positives, full of inspirational quotes made by famous people. I find opening it randomly and reading one quote a day works well for me.

I now found myself in the middle of a wonderfully frightening transition. I had left my counselling and was pleased to have got to this stage, but I was also terrified by the prospect of coping on my own. Like a fledgling all grown up, ready to spread its wings and leave the nest, only, it all looks so vast out there and I didn't know which direction to go in!

It can be hard sometimes to differentiate between fear and excitement; I think it's helpful to have a bit of both. It's normal for me to feel a certain level of trepidation. Counselling has been a big part of my life. Even now, it's like I've been walking a tight rope and all of a sudden, they've took my safety net away!

Two years of counselling taught me a lot of coping techniques. I now have a few additional methods, which are giving me the positive reinforcement I need right now. I have a mantra which I repeat to myself every day, even more so when I'm in situations that make me anxious.

Some of the most common mantras are listed below:

I am what I am.
Action conquers fear.
I am enough.
This too shall pass.
I love and approve of myself.
Keep calm and carry on.
I breathe in calmness and breath out nervousness.
Keep your head up and your heart open.

Obviously, these are just a few, it's what works best for each individual. You might want to change some words around to better suit your situation or you might choose to invent a completely new saying that is unique to you. When I'm stressed, I repeat the phrase 'Nil Nil and all is well', when I'm about to start a table tennis match and the umpire says Nil Nil, I manage to switch off all other distractions and just focus on the job in hand. This inner calm has proven helpful when trying to accomplish any given task.

One thing I miss about my counsellor is the constant reassurance she gave me. Helping me realise I was on the right track, and that I actually had a lot to offer. The way I've chosen to emulate this, is by writing pages of positive reminders that relate to different situations. For example, if I'm about to go out with friends and I'm feeling anxious, I look at a certain page in my notebook, which emphasises that I'm well liked and good company, that I've no need to rehearse or force conversations. Instead, I should just be myself and go with the flow. 'Relax! Your friends have known you for ages and still want to spend time with you, so you're obviously doing something right.' 'Stop agreeing to everything! Your opinion matters too.'

These simple scripts help me with continuing to leave the house and manage my everyday life. As time goes on, and I continue to be more assured and comfortable in my own skin, I hope, I will need to read them less and less.

Some of the other methods which may help you could include cooking or baking, swimming, gardening, walking your dog, music, arts, and crafts or whatever your passion happens to be. Providing it can be used as a positive distraction, it doesn't really matter.

Having a variety of methods open to you has got to be of benefit.

My illness thrives on loneliness, or boredom. The more time I have on my hands, the more I allow the dark thoughts to enter my head. Keeping occupied is one of the greatest weapons in the fight against depression.

ASKING FOR HELP

Confused, lost and in a state of total despondency, I had given up all hope; there didn't seem any point anymore. My whole world felt to be collapsing around me, it was like being in quicksand, the more I struggled the more I was dragged further down. Wrapped in misery and hurting like I'd never hurt before, I just wanted it all to stop, and it's no exaggeration when I say, I yearned for the slow release of death.

What had started with me feeling a bit down, soon escalated into an extremely unhealthy existence of never leaving the house and refusing to interact with anyone. Even talking to my family drained me. To put it simply, I thought I was a burden with nothing to offer, and I really didn't want to be here anymore.

Fast-forward to now, and miraculously, I'm almost the polar opposite of this, unrecognisable, you might say. Don't get me wrong, I still have far to go, I continue to suffer daily with my depression, which at its worst can still be unbearable. The difference is that back then the wretched torment was relentless, were as now, the clouds sometimes part and let me see glimpses of sunshine. In these moments' life is worth living, I savour all the beautiful things that have previously passed me by. I'm much more compassionate towards myself. The self-deprecating me of the past becomes a distant memory. Instead, it is replaced by a newfound appreciation for everything I've got and a positive optimism for things to come.

Before, I didn't see any kind of future, and now it feels like every day's a bonus. Looking forward to birthdays and Christmases to come and excited about all the new experiences I'm going to have.

So, how can a dramatic change like this take place in such a short period of time? Well to answer that question, it has been 5 years now, since my first suicide attempt, and It's been far from easy to get to this stage. It's a process that wouldn't ever have been possible, without me first asking for help.

I know there'll be people reading this who refuse to believe such a change could possibly take place. People who are in a terrible place themselves, have reached rock bottom and feel they have nothing left to live for. They probably find it hard to believe I was ever in their shoes, that I was ever in a suicidal state. I get this attitude, I really do, but to these people I beg you not to give up. Dig deep and try to find whatever fight you've got left. **Please ask for help**! If you've reached the stage that I did, and convinced yourself there's no other way out, then what have you got to lose? Go to see your doctor. You'll be surprised by how understanding they are, and how much help is available to you. Depression is a serious illness that affects millions of people and that is why there's so much help out there. Accepting you've got it is the first stage and was the hardest part for me. I know you're in a dark, scary place at present, but I assure you what you're feeling is not abnormal. It might not seem like it, but all the symptoms, such as low self-esteem, panic and anxiety, extreme changes in your emotional state and generally feeling like crap! They're all part of the illness and like any major illness, it needs treating. **You deserve the help, so please ask for it**!

You will be amazed by how, having someone to talk to, will be of huge benefit. I was extremely pessimistic about going to see a counsellor, but now I can see, it quite literally saved my life. Opening up can take a long time or in some cases happen straight away, but counsellors are used to this and will be patient and empathic towards you. Once I did begin to unload, all my bottled-up emotions came flooding out, and I felt a massive sense of relief.

Once you agree to get help, you're going to come across all the usual spiel from different people involved in your care. If I had a pound for every time, I've been told to be kind to myself and take one small step at a time, I'd be a rich man! You'll get sick of people saying these things, but the reason why they're repeated so often is because it's actually great advice!

When you're depressed, it's so easy to focus on the things you're not good at, instead of all the things that you are. One of my favourite quotes is by Albert Einstein and it illustrates the point I'm trying to make. He says:

'We are all geniuses. But if you judge a fish by its ability to climb a tree, it will spend its entire life thinking it's stupid.'

To me, Penguins are a good example of this. Whilst on the ground they can look awkward, waddling around and slipping on their bellies, but once in the water a magical transformation takes place, as they become brilliant acrobats, effortlessly gliding through the water.

Everyone has something to offer. Depression is an illness that is manageable with the right support, but believe me when I say, asking for help did not come easy to me. Having visited the doctors twice in five years, and one of those times was for some holiday vaccinations! It took me some time to come to terms with the idea of having a fortnightly slot, but I finally accepted that having spent most of my life caring for others and putting them first, it was now time to focus on my own needs.

I am now much better at asking for help when I need it, but frustratingly, I still choose not to if I can possibly help it, this shows that although improving, my self-worth is still a bit fragile. In other words, I continue struggling with the concept, that I'm deserving of support.

I understand that you might not be ready to talk openly about your mental health. It's hard enough talking to a health professional about it, let alone anyone else!

I regularly get asked what I do for a living. Anyone who has a mental health illness and is out of work, will tell you that this is one of the questions they dread the most. You can either choose to answer honestly and say you're not working right now due to your mental health, or you can choose to make something up. You could even have a bit of fun and say that you're a brain surgeon! Joking apart, if you're not ready to share about your illness, and telling a little white lie helps avoid having an uncomfortable conversation, then I don't see an issue with this. I hid my illness for a long time, and although I can see it wasn't healthy to do so, it was necessary at the time. when I was struggling to accept my own illness, I always did this, and even had a rehearsed script for such occasions (one more believable than being a brain surgeon!)

I'm now much better at giving an honest answer. Normally when I give the reason as my mental health, people say they're sorry to hear that and then promptly change the subject! You see, even though mental health is now widely recognised, for many it's still an uncomfortable subject, and I appreciate this. Often, I'm grateful, because it means I don't have to go into detail. Others have surprised me with their responses. It's amazing how many people have had issues with anxiety and depression. It's often the people you would least expect, that share their stories and are able to relate to what you're going through.

NO SHAME

Please don't be ashamed of your mental health. I'm not suggesting you stand up and shout it from the roof tops, but at the same time, don't suffer in silence.

I spent my entire high school years desperately trying to fit into a group, but never quite achieving it. Well now, for the first time in my life I belong to a club, and it's a big one! It's called the mental health club, At least one in four of us are in it, but for some reason it doesn't feel to be anywhere near that number. Every thing's hush-hush, people don't want to admit they're part of it. Sure, there are lots of great support groups out there, but the majority of people are still hiding. I appreciate this is completely their own choice and there may be mitigating circumstances. They may be struggling to accept they're ill in the first place (I know it took me a while!). But if the reason is down to shame, why be ashamed of being in the biggest club in the world?

Compared to other conditions

A friend of mine has type two diabetes and is insulin dependent. she has to inject herself every morning and her insulin needs to be stored in a fridge. This is a particularly important issue when traveling long distance or going on holidays. Due to her condition, she must be extremely careful with her diet and has certain limitations. She needs to do regular gentle exercise, but over exertion can be harmful. She manages her condition very well, part of this involves refusing to do activities that may be detrimental to her health. She has no problem explaining that her Diabetes is the reason for this.

My mother is registered disabled due to chronic back problems, caused by an accident at work several years ago. Just like my friend, she manages her condition well and is still able to live a fulfilled life. If someone asks her to do something which is beyond her capabilities and will be a risk to her health, she has no problem refusing, giving her disability as the reason why.

I think I speak for most people who suffer with their mental health, when I say It's not easy for us to do the same. I find myself coming up with the most elaborate excuses imaginable, to get myself out of situations I can't manage due to my health. Admittedly part of this is to avoid having to explain, but it's mainly because I've felt ashamed. My mum doesn't have to explain, she can just say "I can't because of my bad back" so why can't I be similarly frank about my health. After all, as I've said, I'm in the biggest club in the world! So, millions of people will understand, and for those people who don't, how can we ever expect them too, if we're not upfront and honest about the way we're feeling.

I'm getting better at giving my mental health as a genuine reason why I can't do certain things, but I accept I still have a way to go. It's not easy, but when you start sharing, you realise there's so many people just like you, suddenly you feel less alienated, and you might even make them feel better too!

Remember showing vulnerability is not a weakness, other people will gain strength from your courage in coming forward. Gradually, as I've grown more accepting of my illness, it has become easier for me to be honest about the way I'm feeling. I now choose to involve as many people as I can. The more that know about my illness and its effects, the fewer awkward questions I'm likely to face. Of course, this only works if you've got a supportive group around you, people you can really trust. In this respect I am extremely fortunate.

Try to remember it's not a crime to ask for help. If you have somewhere to go or just want to get out for a little while, there's no shame in asking someone to go with you. everybody needs a bit of a prop from time to time. If the only way you're leaving the house is to be accompanied, then so be it, it's better than staying in and feeling sorry for yourself.

Graded exposure

Sometimes if you picture a full-length journey somewhere, or focus on a task in its entirety, it can soon become overwhelming. Therefore, a good idea is to break things down into more manageable segments. This is where Graded exposure comes in, as a productive tool to help you get your independence back. Imagine having to go 1 mile for an appointment at the doctors. Someone with anxiety issues, may not view this as possible, in fact, in my experience, it may feel a long way off being possible! But instead of focusing on getting to the doctors, this is when you need to simplify things. For starters, concentrate on getting to the end of the street, do not rush yourself. Once you've mastered this you can look towards the next checkpoint ahead, walk a little further and you'll reach the main road at the bottom of the hill, it's shorter distance than you've managed so far, so you should be fine. Once here, you can see the garage in the near distance, also known as checkpoint 3! it's a straight line and less than 5 minutes away. In three manageable steps you have made it to the garage and now you can see the sandwich shop in the distance, with a little endeavor, you will have made it to checkpoint 4! (Obviously, your checkpoints will be different to this, just make sure the distance between them is challenging, but not unattainable). Now you've passed the halfway mark, it would take you just as long to go back home, so you might as well continue! By sticking to these achievable goals, you will be surprised by how far you can get. Always make sure you have a back-up though, somebody available to phone for help in case you need it. In my case I had a Carer who took me out. If you haven't got this option or find yourself on a waiting list, a close friend or family member is a suitable alternative. For a long period, I couldn't leave my house due to my anxiety levels. First and foremost, I wanted to be able to get to the local shop on my own to get necessities and avoid having to rely so much on other people. The shop is a ten-minute walk away (I don't drive). We split the journey up into 6 checkpoints. For the first few weeks we kept repeating the journey together, but then eventually I managed to meet my carer at the first checkpoint. Over time, I was able to go further distances on my own, until eventually I achieved my goal. I have achieved larger challenges since, including getting to the local swimming baths and playing table tennis in the league. All of which I have done through graded exposure.

It's not surprising we find it so difficult to share our mental health stories. The British culture is naturally a reserved one. People find shame in many aspects of life, and often pretend to be something they're not, in order to meet what they deem as societies expectations. I for one, want to do my small part in changing this. And so, embarrassment aside, here goes!

On a Saturday night, I love nothing more than sitting in front of the tele with a lager in my hand, watching 'match of the day', normally whilst shouting abuse at the referee and cursing my team for not scoring enough goals. Some might call this laddish behaviour, but I won't, as I don't want to be accused of sexism! Earlier in the evening I'd watch a romantic comedy starring Jenifer Aniston, I must admit I do like a good rom-com. I'd follow this by watching my favourite couples on 'strictly come dancing' (hardly the most masculine of programs!)

I like watching 'top gear' but I'm also a big fan of 'the great British bake-off'. I enjoy watching the soaps such as 'Coronation Street' but also like series such as 'The Sopranos' 'Killing Eve' or 'the walking dead'- a bloodthirsty program about flesh eating zombies. I think of this as being unusual but maybe it's not. Maybe it's just unusual that I admit to having such random taste. I'm sure there's lots of closet fans out there who secretly watch 'X factor' on a Saturday night and then tell their friends that they'd never watch such rubbish!

I am a sensitive, giving person, but equally at times I can come across as resolute and unyielding. You could describe some of my traits, as being masculine but it's also fair to say I have a number of feminine qualities. In the past I've enjoyed a night out with the lads, drinking pints and propping up the bar, but I've had just as much fun being out with the girls drinking cocktails and dancing the night away. I'm sorry if this is coming across as stereotyping, it just happens to be how it is for me with my friends. The truth is I'm able to contribute well to both sets of groups, but don't find myself a perfect match to either.

The happiest people in life are those who couldn't care less what others think of them. Having their own unique identity and never being ashamed of who they are. This is the sort of person I'm striving to become more like, although, I still have a long way to go.

Imagine the toughest scariest looking guy you can, someone built like a bodybuilder with muscles growing out of his muscles! With a permanent threatening scowl on his face, and a demeaner that says 'don't mess with me or else! Who would have thought this menacing looking guy would be secretly into decorating fairy cakes and flower arranging!

The sad reality is that I know people like this, who would hide such guilty pleasures in a desperate attempt to keep up their macho persona. Who are so terrified of other people's judgement, they keep secret, the things that they love to do the most? Going back to our menacing looking friend, why would he be so reluctant to share his passions? There's nothing there to be ashamed of after all, and it would only be a narrow-minded person who thought any differently. The fact that he has these hidden depths makes him so much more intriguing. I play table tennis in the local league, I'm ashamed to say I kept this fact from past girlfriends, as I presumed, they'd laugh at me. One, I didn't tell for 6 months! I even invented a night school college course, to explain where I was every Wednesday night. Looking back now, I cannot believe what lengths I went too.

I've spent most of my life attempting to fit in with certain groups of people. You could say I've failed miserably at this, or you could say that it's took me until now to realize that it's perfectly ok to be different, in fact it's great to be an individual. If everyone were the same, the world would be an extraordinarily dull place. Sometimes the best thing you can do is accept that you're unique and stop trying so hard to be something you're not. This is a brave thing to do, and people will envy you for it, they might even wish they were more like you themselves.

CHALLENGING YOURSELF

What does having a routine mean to you?
Do you find routine boring?
Do you find it comforting?
Do you feel it's holding you back?
Do you find it a necessity?
Do you desperately need it for your survival?

For someone like me who suffers badly with anxiety, having a steady routine and therefore knowing exactly what I'm doing, is vital. A solid routine helps me to feel safe. That being said, even I like to mix it up from time to time, and I recognise the importance of doing this. Staying in your comfort zone is all well and good, but if I stayed in mine all the time, I'd never leave the house! Pushing yourself a little further, allows you to experience so much more, and ultimately leads to living a more fulfilled life. I know all this to be true, but it's still easier said than done.

Having an element of routine and the structure that comes with this, seems to me to be the sensible way to approach life. But I've always been an excessive planner, even before my mental health issues. I'm the sort of person who likes to know what's around the next corner, both literally and figuratively speaking. Whereas some people might enjoy the element of surprise, I deeply fear it! Some might see this as a tad obsessive, but then again most of you don't have an anxiety disorder to contend with. Much depends on what hardships you've faced in life and how many mental scars you've been left with.

Sports men and woman can be extremely obsessive with their routines. Some of their superstitions can seem ludicrous to most of us. Anything from having a lucky pair of socks, to lining their water bottles up in a precise order. These acts might seem odd, but we all share in having such idiosyncrasies- just perhaps to a lesser extent. Let us take an everyday thing like having a shower. Without even realising it, you will automatically do things in a certain order, and it would feel strange to do things any differently.

When I get out of the shower, I always start by drying my feet first and then working my way up my body, eventually drying my chest and arms, and finishing with my head. Many people may think this to be extremely odd, they might in fact, do it in the completely opposite order to me. It might make more sense to dry your hair first to stop it dripping everywhere, but I'm bald on top, so don't have that problem! Anyway, whatever your preferred method is, I bet you've done it the same way for as long as you can remember. If you try altering this routine, even slightly, it will completely throw you out of sync. It might even ruin the whole experience! The fact is, we all take comfort in routine to a certain degree.

You've all heard of the saying, *'practice makes perfect'*. A repetitive routine can be used as a legitimate learning method, as the more you do something the more automatic it becomes. Bruce lee put it well when he said, *'Don't fear the man that knows 10,000 kicks, fear the one that knows 1 kick but has practiced it 10,000 times!'*

Driving a car is also a good example. Most drivers would tell you that in their first couple of driving lessons, nothing felt natural, everything was like an alien concept to them, and they couldn't imagine being able to drive on their own. But then, with much perseverance and repetition, what seemed like an impossible feat, not only became possible, but soon became second nature to them. This exact same mind-set can be applied when facing any challenges.

Shoot for the moon, even if you miss, you'll land among the stars! Challenge yourself to get the most pleasure out of life.

Personally, I think it's important to face up to your demons and test yourself daily. Whilst doing this you need to continue looking after yourself and be accepting of the limitations caused by your mental health. It's all about finding the right balance for you.

My daily challenges can include, walking to the corner shop on my own, going to the supermarket with family, picking up mail from my old house, forcing myself to have a social chat with a friend, answering the telephone or front door. These last two might seem a bit trivial to some, but they can be the most difficult, especially if I don't know who's on the other end of the line or behind the door. It's the fear of the unknown that often prevents me from being able to do this. My home is my sanctuary, but it's so easy to become trapped. Don't let isolation become your friend. I'm all for protecting yourself and keeping safe, but not if it means you're sacrificing experiencing life.

'Action may not always bring happiness, but there is no happiness without action' (Benjamin Disraeli)

I began visiting the town centre once a week with my mother, even though I was extremely anxious on the day and in the build up to it, I still forced myself to do it. To be honest with you, I didn't enjoy any part of this experience, but I viewed it as a necessary infliction. If you're like me and you fear busy places, I don't think there's any harm in steering clear of them as much as you can. However, in life you can't guarantee avoiding places such as town centres, indefinitely. There will be times in the future when you have no choice. I attempt to make such times less stressful by remaining well practiced. So, I don't put myself through the rigger for no reason, there is method in my madness!

'Live all you can; it's a mistake not to. It doesn't matter what you do in particular, so long as you have had your life. If you haven't had that, what have you had?' (Henry James)

I say, just keep putting one foot in front of the other and you won't go far wrong!

Even walking short distances on my own is a big challenge. But once I feel comfortable with a certain route, I try to increase the distance. This must be done gradually, as too much too soon can result in a panic attack and send me right back to square one. As well as distance, I also work on the following:

Slowing down- It might sound a simple thing to do but for me it's not. Due to my anxiety I tend to race from A to B in record speed, all so I can get back to the safety of my home. The walk itself should be a pleasant experience, I just need to remind myself to take my time and appreciate the journey.

Keeping pace- If someone is in front of me walking at a slower pace, I will slow down to avoid catching them up. Equally if someone's behind me walking faster I will quicken up. Allowing someone to walk past me is a huge challenge. Sitting on a bench and having several people walk past me is extremely daunting, but something I try hard to achieve.

Being sociable- When I'm out walking with my friends, I'm a completely different person. I always smile and say hello to people passing by, on occasions I might even enter into a conversation. When on my own, walking past the same people in exactly the same kind of location, I don't say a word! Shoulders slumped and head down, I don't even risk eye contact. This is providing I haven't found an alternative path or crossed the street. And so, a big challenge for me, is to keep my shoulders up and my head high, acknowledging fellow pedestrians as I go. This of course is easier said than done and completely depends on the day.

Repetition is the key, just like anything, if you do something regularly enough, the task will become easier and less intimidating. Often the anticipation is far worse than the actual event.

It's all about taking one manageable step at a time, as opposed to giant unrealistic leaps! This is especially relevant if you have a mental health illness and you're in a vulnerable, unpredictable state of mind. A friend of mine, who's battled her mental health all her life, told me that when her illness is at its worst, her daily challenges can involve simply getting out of bed, and getting washed and dressed. I can appreciate this, as depression tightens its grip over me, even the simplest of tasks can take great effort and I too have days when getting out of bed proves impossible. You can't see the point of doing anything anymore- including washing and dressing. But it's important to keep challenging yourself, however small and pointless these challenges may seem. This same lady is now able to travel the country on her own, giving inspirational talks in rooms full of people, she continues to spread much needed awareness and fills me with hope for my future. She has proven to me that anything is possible, but who knows if she'd have ever reached this stage, if she hadn't continued challenging herself, even in her darkest hours. Somehow, I doubt she would.

INSPIRATIONS AND PERSONAL PRIDE

Having people who inspire you is extremely important for your mental health; they can give you the motivation and positive reinforcement needed to achieve your goals. My main inspirations are friends and family; however, I'm also inspired by many sports men and women. There are several bad things highlighted on the news every day. Tragic events happening all over the world, and often closer to home with terrorist attacks over the recent years. If you're like me and you already suffer with your anxiety, such events can influence you leaving the house, as you don't feel safe to do so. It's hard, I know, but this is when it's important that we also remember all the positive events taking place. I use my inspirations to help me do this.

Everyone loves a good underdog story, someone who has achieved great things against all the odds.

This Egyptian Paralympian (Ibrahim Hamadtou) was told that he could never play table tennis as he had no arms or stumps to grip the bat. He proved that with single mindedness and remarkable determination, anything is possible! Most of the athletes involved have had to endure massive setbacks in their lives, setbacks that would cause the average person to lose all hope. These amazingly heroic people fight so hard and perform incredible feats to prove all the doubters wrong.

The Paralympic moto is '**Yes I Can**'. I'm sad to say that most of the time mine is 'No I Can't!' I find myself blaming my depression for this, but sometimes it's just a convenient excuse. When I'm playing sports my competitive spirit shines through, if only I could view depression as my latest opponent, maybe I could put it in its place! Seeing my inspirations and their

175

achievements, gives me a huge boost and makes me want to try harder to emulate their success.

Inspirations- achieving greatness

I know it's sad to have a picture of yourself on your bedroom wall, but it does have a positive purpose. The person pictured next to me is a professional darts player called James Wade. The thing we both have in common, is that we have won tournaments whilst battling our mental health illnesses. James is one of the best darts players in the world, whereas I play table tennis in local leagues. James suffers with bipolar and had to have time away from the sport due to his illness. I too had to have a year out from playing in the league when my anxiety levels reached their highest peak and I struggled to function properly.

James is ranked number 6 in the world and is an extremely talented player, he also comes across as a genuinely nice guy, he's always respectful of his opponents and conducts himself well, win or lose. When I watch him on the stage, he appears very comfortable and in his comfort zone, but off the stage doing interviews, and even on his walk on, I can see a lot of myself in him. Frailties such as low self-esteem, looking awkward and nervous, like he wants to be anywhere else. That is why, it's truly remarkable that with such obvious confidence issues, He's still able to perform to such a high standard in front of thousands of noisy fans, not to mention the millions watching on sky sports! For this reason, I admire him more than any other sportsman.

Going back to the pictures on my wall. They're the first thing I see when I get up in a morning and I use them as a positive message to start the day. They remind me that anything is possible, and I can still achieve good things despite of my illness. Whether your inspirations are well known celebrities or friends and family, doesn't matter. What matters is that you use them as a positive influence in moving forward and becoming the best version of yourself.

As someone suffering with depression, I must admit, I've become a bit of a defeatist and very good at putting myself down. This can soon result in feelings of total incompetence. That's why it's vital to keep reminding myself that I am good at things, and not to shy away from my successes. None of us find it easy to blow our own trumpet. The majority of us are naturally modest and sometimes find it a challenge to self-praise.

I remember once at a staff team-building day, we were all asked to write down one positive thing about ourselves. We were each given a large sheet of jotter paper with our names at the top and five minutes to do this, and then pin our sheets to the wall. I went totally blank and devoid of any ideas. Five minutes went by and I was beginning to feel extremely awkward. If the exercise were to write negative comments, I could have easily filled the whole page. I was troubled by how such a simple task was proving to be so difficult. So, I looked around the room for inspiration. Amazingly what I saw were lots of empty pieces of paper and everyone else looking equally bemused. In the end we all had to be given extra time to complete the task. Once we had all finished, the idea was to go around the room and add a positive thing to each other's list. This proved to be a much easier proposition, and soon, we all had sheets of paper full up with our best qualities.

Later that day I was able to sit down and read all the kind things my colleagues had written about me. I couldn't get over how popular I was. I felt quite emotional and humbled by it all, it acted as a huge boost to my self-esteem. It's so easy to put yourself down and forget all the great things other people see in you.

Due to my illness, I now have major confidence issues, which unfortunately dictate how I live my life. On getting up in a morning, my aim is to safely maneuver myself through the day until it's time to go to bed again. If I have to leave the house this challenge dramatically increases, as my safety becomes a higher risk. It's a big world out there with many potential threats and I feel much more comfortable keeping in my little bubble.

I do challenge myself to get out, but due to my anxiety levels, it takes considerably more planning than it would for the average person. This is the only way I'm able to function at the moment, but it's essential I don't forget that life hasn't always been this way and won't always be like this in the future. I haven't always been such a shy and nervous person.

In the past, I've done such things as a best man speech, where I had to stand in a room full of people and try to be humorous! I have spoken eulogies at funerals, which if anybody's had to do, will know is far from easy.

179

At work I was always chosen to be the staff spokesperson, not because I was particularly outspoken (although some might argue that point!) but because people could rely on me to tactfully get our point across at management meetings. I was never too bolshie but at the same time, I didn't have a problem standing up for what the team believed in. Due to these qualities, I was selected to be a representative for all our health care assistants at a pay structure meeting. This was whilst working for the NHS. I had to prepare and give a speech to a panel of managers I'd never met before. A daunting prospect to say the least. My efforts resulted in over thirty members of staff going up from band 2 to band 3 workers and the obvious benefits of a higher salary. At the time people were able to put their full trust in me and had confidence that I wouldn't crumble under pressure. This is why I was chosen, and also why I didn't have to buy a round in the pub, for several weeks to come!

In contrast to that, right now you couldn't even rely on me to walk to the corner shop to buy a loaf of bread. Some days, there's a strong possibility, I won't muster enough courage to leave the house on my own. My own expectations and those of others have somewhat diminished lately and I often feel like a shadow of my old self. It's fair to say, the goal posts have shifted and my aims in life are more centred around the present, rather than looking too far ahead. This is a necessity, with my mental state being so precarious.

Even though I can get extremely frustrated with the situation, I try not to. It's just how things are at the moment, and I tell myself it's only going to be like this temporary. If you are battling your mental health and your progress seems slow, the chances are you're doing better than you think. Nobody notices the grass growing when they sit and stare at it, but sure enough it grows, or else you wouldn't need to keep mowing it! Trust me when I say, you are doing well. Remember too, to celebrate your achievements, even if they seem small compared to your past accomplishments. If anything, there more significant now than back then, a time when you didn't have depression to contend with.

I met a friend the other day and he was buzzing because he'd just got a big promotion at work. I was delighted for him, but also happy that I'd managed to walk into Aldi by myself and buy a loaf of bread, an equally huge achievement for me! I wasn't going to mention it, because it seemed insignificant in comparison, but I did, and he was really pleased for me. We celebrated both achievements together.

In table tennis I don't lose very often. Right now, my depression is my main opponent and I'm positive I'll beat it and achieve great things again in the future.

STRENGTH IN NUMBERS

Battling your mental health is tough but made easier with strength in numbers. It's easy to pre-empt how you think others view you and your illness, but I must admit, most of the time I've been completely wrong with each of my presumptions.

A MOTHER'S PERSPECTIVE

My mum wrote the following passage and I thank her for her honesty.

When a new-born baby is put into your arms there's a special bond that can't be broken and as they grow it doesn't wane at all. A maternal instinct is an extremely powerful thing, as most mothers would confirm.

From the very first moment of their lives your protection instinct kicks in and you're lost in admiration of the tiny infant in your care. All you want to do is protect them from harm, in any way that you can but life is sadly not like that and there are times when there is nothing you can do to take their pain away.

As they grow your concerns are always there as you want the very best for them, and when they go to school, you leave them at the gates with feelings of trepidation.

Letting go has always been a difficult thing for me and both of my sons would probably tell you that I wear my heart on my sleeve and whenever one of my siblings hurts, I hurt too.

It has therefore been an excruciating time to see one of them struggling with health issues without understanding or being able to help. Broken bones can be easily fixed and although traumatic at the time, they can soon be forgotten by all concerned. Other childhood illnesses often cause a certain amount of sleepless nights but generally don't take too long to get over.

An illness that cannot be categorised in a straightforward way, seems much more frightening and difficult to comprehend for all concerned. The only way to help I find is to be there for them when they need you. There's a fine line between helping and hindering and I have to admit that there are times when I feel that I get it slightly wrong, but I try to learn from my mistakes. Sometimes having a stranger in your midst is not easy to accept, as your son is hidden from view quite a lot due to the illness, which envelops him.

When I see glimpses of him returning, be it a smile that isn't forced or a mischievous glint in his eyes, I know that he's going to be all right.

Sometimes you can be so wrapped up in your own personal battles that you forget how your health issues are affecting your loved ones. Living with depression, is not only hard for you but also difficult for those most close to you. I get questions posted to me all the time, from people desperate for advice on how to help someone they love, who has a mental health illness. Yes, it's hard for them, but believe me, it would be even harder and more painful if you excluded them all together.

It troubles me when I read my mother describing it as, sometimes like living with a stranger, but I guess that's the reality now. I can be quite distant at times and when I'm feeling down, I don't always manage to hide it.

Desperately wanting to help someone but not knowing how to go about it must be extremely frustrating. What's Important to remember is, often just being there for us can be hugely beneficial.

Brotherly Love?

The first time my brother witnessed me having a panic attack, we were in a busy farm shop. Before this I'd felt my anxiety rising. In truth, I just wanted to get the hell out as quickly as possible. Unfortunately, there were factors that prevented this. Firstly, there appeared to be queues everywhere and I wasn't sure which one we should be in. Secondly my brother was in a slow chilled out mode and wanting to browse the store! Of course, he had no idea of my urgency to escape and the pending doom that was now suffocating me. Instead, he said, 'calm down, what's up with you!' and even began to laugh. He presumed I was playing some practical joke on him. It wasn't until I was bent over hyperventilating that he realized it was no joke. I didn't blame him for his reaction, you can't expect someone to immediately understand, if they've never seen you like this. Later, outside in the car park he was extremely apologetic and needed plenty of reassurance that I was alright.

Obviously, now it's different. He doesn't make a big deal of it, but also knows that me having a panic attack whilst we're out, is always a possibility. The same goes for my friends who are all aware of my illness. At first, I chose to suffer it in silence and not include people. My panic attacks have become less frequent of late, as I have learnt several coping methods and know what situations to try and avoid. People being aware, alleviates some of my anxieties, as they're no longer shocked by me, instead they know how to respond in a helpful manner. This can include keeping calm and getting me to fresh air or a quieter environment. Using mirroring techniques to help me control my breathing. Most importantly, they're able to offer copious amounts of reassurance, which is precisely what I need in these terrifying moments.

A smile hides our true emotions.

Only my immediate family and closest friends can see behind my mask. I am capable of convincing the rest of the world that I'm fine when the reality is – I'm anything but!

I couldn't attend my grandma's funeral due to my anxiety issues. My immediate family know the reason for this, but other friends and family were simply told I wasn't well on the day. In truth, I would never have coped in that environment, a building with only one door, makes me feel completely trapped. I would have had major problems being sat on the front row, which of course was the furthest from the entrance/exit, not to mention all those people in such a confined space. I weighed up all the pros and cons and eventually concluded, that me freaking out and having a major meltdown right in the middle of the crematorium, was not going to be helpful to anyone! Instead, I had a close friend take me to my grandma's favourite park and let me say goodbye to her in my own special way. We did this whilst the service was taking place.

FRIENDSHIP

It's so great to have a best friend. In my case it's like having an extension to my family. I've known Tim since I was six years old. We have grown up together sharing many great experiences, as well as some heartaches. Friends in and out of school, girlfriends, buying first houses, family troubles, family holidays, lad's holidays, weddings, funerals, Tim becoming a dad. We have always been there for each other, through all the highs and lows, all the celebrations and disappointments, and I can honestly say I couldn't wish for a better pal.

From a young age we've always been open and honest with each other. If I ever had any major concerns in life, I would go speak to Tim, and I'd like to think he's always done the same with me. Due to this, we both know each other inside out and know some very personal things, which few others ever will. We've developed a special bond and familiarity. Instinctively knowing how each other's feeling and if there is something wrong. In short, I would literally trust him with my life.

I know that in reading this he will be embarrassed by my words of kindness, but I'm afraid he'll have to put up with them, because I genuinely love him like a brother, and only ever want the best for him and his family.

Tim was aware of my depression and anxiety problems but was not aware of the extent of it. This was extremely hard for me, as I was so used to sharing all my concerns with him. But how can you possibly tell your best friend, that you're feeling so low you don't want to be here anymore. That's a difficult thing to tell anyone, let alone, someone with such an emotional attachment. Therefore, I chose to keep it from him and from the rest of my family. I had to tell someone though, so chose to open up to my counsellor.

Several months later I was out for a walk with Tim, I hadn't intended for today to be the day that I told him everything, but maybe subconsciously it's exactly what I needed to do. I accidently let something slip about being visited by the crisis team. Before I knew it, I was telling him everything. My whole emotions came pouring out, any thoughts of protecting my friend from the truth had now gone, it was too late for that. I know it must sound selfish, but the main thing I felt was an amazing sense of relief. No more pretense, everything was now out in the open. His initial response was one of anger, which surprised me. I don't know why it surprised me, but it did. I guess I'd thought a lot about how my loved ones would react to my death. I thought they'd be sad, and they might try to blame themselves in some way. One thing I didn't consider, was them being pissed off with me! But it's a perfectly reasonable response, to what they may view as a selfish act.

I tried telling Tim that it was no big deal, and the world could survive without one more person in it. This only fueled his anger further. *"No big deal! It couldn't be any bigger deal! Have you even considered how it would affect your family? How it would affect me?"* Next came an awkward silence for the remainder of the walk. It's funny, because Tim is one of the few people, I can normally sit in comfortable silence with, but this was far from comfortable and I half wished the ground would swallow me up.

The next time I saw him he'd had time to absorb everything that I'd told him. He was extremely supportive, as deep down I knew he would be. He said that he hoped I realised I could continue to talk to him about anything, and that he was grateful that I'd chosen him to share such a personal admission. It was a huge risk confiding in him like I did, but it's also a risk I'm really glad I took. We're now as close as we've ever been.

I feel so fortunate to have many amazing friends, too many to mention them all in this book, but I can't fail to mention Peter. Unlike Tim, we didn't grow up together. I met him at work, whilst in my early twenties, we hit it off immediately and have been great friends ever since. We have also gone through a lot of significant events together and developed an incredibly close bond. He knows a great deal about my depression and just like Tim, I would trust him with my life. I know that he would drop everything if I needed him (He has on several occasions) even though just like Tim, he has a young family of his own. He too is an extended version of my family, so much so he calls my mum *'mum'* every time he calls around.

Two years ago, I had to go for a medical to decide whether or not I was entitled to Employment Support

Allowance. For several weeks building up to the day, I was a nervous wreck. It was dominating my life. From getting up in a morning to going to bed at night, it was the only thing on my mind. It had completely taken over everything and I was quite literally petrified by the prospect.

Peter booked the day off work to take me to the medical. It took great endeavour to get me there and whilst there, he somehow managed to keep me relatively calm. Tim booked the day before off to take me out playing golf for the day. This proved to be equally important as he somehow managed to give me a fun day and miraculously took my mind off the medical. There is no way I would have ever got through this day, if it weren't for the support of my fantastic friends. It annoys me when I think about people who are in the same position as me, but who don't have the same support. Without this they may not pluck up the courage to even get themselves to the medical, let alone answer all the questions suitably. Their claim for the benefit could therefore be declined. I wonder how many mentally ill people are out there, who are not receiving what they're entitled to, just because the whole process is too daunting for them.

I have a friend who lives about an hour's car journey away. He visits me once a week to take me out for a walk. He is extremely patient with me, we never make any concrete plans, as he knows a lot depends on how I'm feeling on the day, as to how far we'll be able to go. On occasions we've just gone for a drive. On some occasions I've not been well enough to leave the house. Whatever happens he always understands and has never once complained.

I feel truly blessed to have such selfless people in my life. As I continue to use them as a crutch to lean on, they continue to welcome me back with open arms. I hope they all realise how much I appreciate them.

For those people less fortunate than me, I hope you realise, you are far from alone. My thoughts are always with fellow sufferers, I know this alone is not enough, but there also exists many organisations that will be of help. Through your doctors or charities such as MIND, you will be able to access all the great services out there and meet many likeminded people. This can be done through support groups which exist in your local area, or if you're like me and you can't get to such places, online support groups or befriending services, can be just as beneficial. Your doctor will refer you to the service that best meets your needs. All this process will happen gradually, you will not be rushed or pushed into anything you're not comfortable with.

People have a powerful influence over other people, they can create both positive experiences and negative ones. As a youngster, you're highly impressionable, no one can argue that your upbringing has a significant impact on the person you end up becoming. But I think even as an adult you can be easily manipulated to think or react in a certain manner. Your working lives can, therefore, be equally significant. I'm a caring person, but the fact that I've done it for a living and always worked in female dominated jobs, has, if anything enhanced my sensitive side and made me more considerate to those around me. When your one of the few blokes, outnumbered by all those women, it pays to be respectful! My best mate Tim on the other hand, has worked in male dominated factory environments. The comparison between both is immeasurable. In Tim's line of work if you didn't swear every other word, you'd stand out as being extremely odd, and you'd risk becoming alienated. What would be seen in my workplace, as unacceptable derogatory comments, in his, would be viewed as good-natured banter. His big challenge has always been remembering to switch off when he returned home to his wife and kids, otherwise he'd risk a whole heap of trouble!

Whether you are an introvert or an extrovert, a follower, or a pioneer, you will spend the largest period of your lives working. During time spent in the workforce, it is difficult not to be influenced by the collective behaviour of your colleagues. Your behaviour may change without you even realizing it.

There's nothing wrong with being a sensitive person, but I sometimes wonder how my life might have mapped out, if I'd chosen an alternative profession. If I'd been pushed to the limit, in an environment outside of my comfort zone. This might have toughened me up and helped me to develop a thicker skin. Maybe I would have been better equipped to cope with the challenges ahead. I might not have developed the same anxiety issues. There's also a strong possibility, that it wouldn't have made any difference whatsoever, as you could argue, the damage had already been inflicted in my five years of hell at high school.

Hindsight's a wonderful thing. Yes, things might have turned out better, but they might have turned out a whole heap worse. It's unhealthy getting bogged down with all the 'What Ifs'.

PERSPECTIVE

I've always been captivated by the wonders of nature. Like the waves crashing against the rocks, spellbinding and magnificent in all their beauty and raw power.

Nature reminds me that we're all just a tiny part of something much greater. Much greater in fact than we can ever fully comprehend. This really helps me to put my issues into perspective.

I don't mean to sound morbid, but the one thing we can all guarantee is that someday we're not going to be here anymore. I'm not afraid of this prospect, but due to recent events and having come close to the edge, I've become more appreciative of life, and I take far less for granted. I now understand that life is less about success and more about personal experiences. After all, when we do die, we can't take anything with us.

I've always been fascinated by wildlife programs, so I'm going to share a few interesting facts with you.

1/ The Peregrine Falcon has eyesight up to 8 times better than an average human being. They can spot another eagle from 50miles away and get there rapidly, with a top speed of 240 mph. even the average birds, ones that you might see every day in your gardens, can reach speeds of 30 mph and each year journey up to 16000 miles in a collective migration!

2/ The Grizzly Bear has a bite that's over 10 times the power of a human one. The shear force could shatter a tenpin bowling ball!

3/ The Ant is tiny, but highly industrious in its colony. They have the strength to lift objects up to 50 times their own body weight. No human could ever come close to matching this feat. It would be the equivalent of lifting a large transit van!

4/ The Sea Wasp Jellyfish is beautiful but deadly. A transparent predator, with venom so potent, it would only take the equivalent amount of a pinch of salt, to kill a full-grown man!

5/ The Zebra can stand within moments of being born, within hours they are running. I believe it to be a similar time scale for horses. It takes the average human baby 12-18 months to accomplish the same feat.

I love watching nature programs and discovering interesting facts such as these. They remind me that we're all just animals after all, and we all have the same right to live on this planet as anything else, no more or no less. We are classed as the superior species, but I sometimes doubt this is true, for one thing we don't have any of the remarkable skills listed above. On top of this, we're the only species who seem determined to destroy each other, not to mention our planet. We are a tiny part of something much greater than any of us can ever fully understand.

If we take things further, when compared to the wonderful vastness of the universe, our planet itself is incomprehensibly small. The biggest in our solar system is Jupiter. You could fit 1300 earths inside it. The sun is 1000 times bigger still, and the solar system itself is a massive 287.46 billion Km in diameter. These numbers may seem astronomical but are completely disproportionate to the size of the universe, in fact our solar system is a mere speck of dust in comparison. It's also just one of a ludicrously high number of others. Every star you see in the night sky is a sun just like ours, with planets orbiting around it.

If you consider the number of grains of sand in our world, including all the great deserts. Multiply this number by ten, and you'll be close to the numbers of stars in the universe. That's 70 thousand million, million, million, or 7 followed by 22 zeros if you prefer!

You might be wondering why I've chosen this section of the book to go all astrophysicist on you! You might also be wondering what on earth it's got to do with mental health. Well, in my opinion, the answer is everything. I for one, find that contemplating the great magnitude of things, helps me to remain grounded.

Being someone who suffers with irrational fears, it also helps me gain some much-needed perspective. As I often sit in my garden, looking up at the night sky, I think about how insignificant we are in comparison and I allow myself to be dwarfed by the enormity of it all. I feel privileged to be the tinniest piece of the great tapestry of life. For the deep thinkers amongst us it's pointless trying to over complicate things, you can spend your whole life searching for answers and end up regretting the time you've wasted! Life is far too short and far too precious to do this.

Who cares if you don't conform to societies expectations, the only opinion that truly counts is your own? What's wrong with being a little different anyway? We are all special in our own way. At the same time though, to counteract that statement, we're all equally insignificant in the grand scheme of things. Hundreds of years from now, people aren't likely to remember what you did in your lifetime. Whether you do good or bad, you're successful or not, it's not really important, as memories of you will evaporate over time. So, with all that in mind, why on earth do we put so much pressure on ourselves?

When you're battling your mental health it's not always easy to see the positive side to anything. Even though your friends might see big improvements, it's hard for you to notice any progress. It's easier to believe that everyone's superior to you. But try to remember, other people have their issues too. Others also struggle with the everyday pressures of life. Nobody's perfect!

Allow yourself to become lost in the vastness of nature. For once, just enjoy being small and pressure free.

Last month I took a rare trip to the town centre, the last time I did this it resulted in a panic attack. I did this with the intention of challenging myself. I was accompanied by my mother. Although I was uncomfortable, to say the least, all was going surprisingly well. We parked in a multi-storey car park which was very busy, and I'd managed to get out of the car which was a great start! Once at the piazza among the shops I was surrounded by people, some walking towards me, some coming at me from behind. A terrifying prospect for me, but one that I was coping with, although admittedly I did considerably tighten my grip on my mums' arm! The next challenge was to go into a shop and buy something (some deodorant I think, but that's not important). This was to prove more problematic. I was doing Ok until the queuing stage, but sadly this was all too much for me, with far too many people in such a small space. I ended up hurrying out of the shop without purchasing anything.

At the time it was all about looking after myself, as I went into survival mode. But then came the feelings of foolishness and failure. I was so disappointed with myself. I'd soon gone from feeling elated, **'look at me, look how well I'm doing'** to feeling overwhelmed and out of my depth. Later that day, once I'd had time to calm down and reflect, I actually felt extremely proud of what I'd achieved. It's all about perspective. Yes, I'd had to leave the shop, but I'd managed to get into town in the first place, which was a major feat in itself. I'd also managed my anxiety well and avoided having a panic attack. All positive steps in the right direction.

I recently played in my local league championships at table tennis. I got to the semi-final stage before losing to the player who went on to win the event. Frustratingly, as good a player as he is, I had beaten him both times we'd played in the league and I really fancied my chances. There were people watching, not many, but enough to make me feel uncomfortable and very self-conscious. On the day I didn't perform, I let nerves get the better of me. But wait a minute, twelve months prior to this I'd had to pull out of playing in the league all together, I wasn't even well enough to come and watch this tournament, let alone play in it.

Just being able to stay in this kind of environment and feel ok for most of the day, was, and is, a huge testament to how far I've come. Again, it's just about putting things in perspective. I managed to get all the way to the semi-final stage which is something to be proud of!

For other people suffering with their mental health, it's important that you try to put your situations into perspective. Try to focus on what you're doing well, as opposed to what you're not. You might struggle to see it now, but there'll be much more positives than you think.

Sometimes it's good to simplify things. Yesterday in the park I witnessed a little boy seeing the water fountain turning on, As the water shot upwards, there was shear magical delight written all over his face, this was followed by an uncontrollable fit of giggles. In seeing this I couldn't help but smile, but then it was tainted by a moment of sadness, as I asked myself, when was the last time I'd laughed like that? Seeing the world through the eyes of a child is a wonderful thing. It's the lack of pretense that I really like, what you see is exactly what you get. If they're happy, the world knows they're happy, and similarly if they're sad, they never hide their emotions. As adults we still have joyful moments, but we rarely allow ourselves to really let go and celebrate them. It's like, we're scared that we'll get judged badly for showing our true emotions. Worried about feeling out of control and drawing attention to ourselves, risking a blemish to our cool steely exterior! I think this is extremely sad, life is so short and will soon pass us all by, so why worry so much about what other people might think.

Channeling our Inner child

We all have an inner child in us fighting to get out, and I think it's important to let him out every so often. To a young child, life is a big adventure. They're fascinated by everything they discover, and they perceive the world in its simplest form. Become an adult and suddenly you lose all that, you notice less, and everything becomes much more complicated. I appreciate that as an adult we have more responsibilities, but as far as complicating things and not following our instincts, I don't think we help ourselves. They say that knowledge is power, but I think in terms of happiness, too much knowledge can be a dangerous thing. As we constantly search for hidden depths in everything, we become more guarded and pessimistic, we soon completely lose the trusting nature we once had as a child.

As adults, are we prohibited from having any fun? Is it a crime to act silly? If it is, I'm afraid I'm guilty as charged! It's easier if you have kids of your own, a bit of tomfoolery is expected. I envy those of my friends who have children. They get to go to the seaside, dive around on the beach playing Frisbee and charge with their arms and legs flaying into the sea. They have the perfect excuse for channeling their inner child. But what's to stop us all doing the same thing? To occasionally lose your inhibitions and completely let go. If you're worried about being locked up! you can always pick your moment or even do something silly in the comfort of your own home.

The other day I went to the park, at a time when I knew it would be quiet and the kids would be in school. I got on one of the swings and started to swing as high as I could. I lead my head right back and pointed my legs straight out in front of me. I could see only sky and I imagined myself flying through the air. I forgot where I was and more importantly, how old I was. The only slight reminder was the fact that I barely fit, and the chains were digging into my sides! Other than that, I got completely lost in the moment and stayed like that for a good half an hour, as I completely lost track of time. If you've took any notice to the rest of this book, you'll realize that half an hour is a long time for me to be in this sort of situation. Normally, I'd have to keep a close eye on my environment and would panic that someone was lurking around the corner, but on this occasion, there was none of that. Being in-tune with my inner child like this, allowed me to feel more relaxed. Young children don't have the same kind of anxieties. It's only as an adult that these insecurities and irrational fears start to mount up.

In the blink of an eye my brother and I have turned into adults, but the two cheeky chaps above still exist in us to this day, and I wouldn't want it any other way.

Why does a dog instinctively want to chase a ball?

Most people are permanently on the edge, highly volatile in their nature and so tightly coiled that they could snap at any given moment. When things are going well, it's in our nature to fear the worst. We're always looking for a hidden agenda, a reason for things to change. Is it possible that subconsciously, we need to find this negative, in an attempt to return to some kind of equilibrium? Is it possible, that we don't like the idea of too much happiness? Why do we always insist on hitting the self-destruct button? Can we even help being this way, or maybe, just like the dog chasing the ball, it's an inbuilt desire that's too powerful to resist. I enjoy delving into the complexities of the human mind, but know, I'll never come close to understanding it. One thing I am certain of, is that a child's approach is far kinder on your mental health. So, in conclusion, don't neglect your inner child, It's a huge and important part of you. I challenge you all to embrace this side and let it out more often.

PART THREE
MY STORY STIGMAS –
THE BENEFIT SYSTEM –
QUESTIONS & ANSWERS

In this final part of the book, I'm going to risk offending a few people, as I challenge some of the stigmas still surrounding mental health and give my opinion of the benefit system as a whole.

I will attempt to tackle the most common and challenging questions, sent to me by fellow sufferers, or by people who want to understand our symptoms better.

TICKING BOXES

FUN AT THE JOB CENTRE

I'm sat for what seems like hours, I glance down at my watch and I'm alarmed to see it's not even been ten minutes yet! Welcome to the job centre, the place where time truly does stand still.

Now imagine the person you'd least like to meet down a dark alley. Built like a brick outhouse, heavily tattooed, crazy looking eyes, and appears like he could crush you with his little finger! He's sat directly across from me, giving me what I can only describe as a death stare. I'm desperately trying to avoid glancing in his direction.

You get used to seeing all the usual crowds, to my left is the single mums club, all congregated together with their army of prams. Normally, they're discussing having more babies and getting their benefits increased. A baby is an excellent prop to have with you in the job centre, as you can get away with so much more. Let's just say you've been a bit slack and not managed to apply for your allocated number of jobs, what are the chances of someone getting mad with you whilst you're cradling an infant. If that infant happens to start crying, that's a bonus, you'll likely get seen and sent away much quicker!

Looking to my right I see the hoodie brigade, some sat, and some stood up, mainly consisting of young lads wearing ridiculously baggy pants that hang down showing half their boxer shorts or worse, sometimes their arse crack! Their faces are part covered, in an attempt to look as menacing as they can. Their conversations consist of bragging about crimes committed and time spent in prison or young offenders' institutions. Two of them are comparing their ankle tags and discussing when their curfews are up. As well as this, they're all ogling the girls at the other side of the room. It feels like a scene from a high school disco!

Also grouped together in the corner is the so-called non-English speakers. These people are very interesting, whilst in the waiting area their English is perfect and they appear to have a larger vocabulary than I do, but as soon as they're sat with one of the advisers, something magically happens to them, all of a sudden, they can't speak two words of it! Another successful tactic implored at the job centre.

Much of the people attending are playing a game of warfare. Those who know the system inside out and exactly what they can and can't get away with. They choose to manipulate and deceive their way through the whole process, hoping to avoid work for as long as they possibly can. I know this because I've heard them discussing tactics in the waiting area! Then you've got the security guards who I'll politely describe as a total joke. There are several signs up throughout the building, saying no food and drink and no use of mobile phones. It's no exaggeration to say, every other person has a chocolate bar or sandwich in one hand, and their mobile in the other. In the middle of all this you have the security, who are blatantly ignoring it all, prancing around in their uniforms, looking important, but not actually doing very much, aside from hugging and high-fiving people that they know!

On the other side of the desks, you have the job advisers, who funnily enough never seem to give any advice! I'm reluctant to badmouth them too much, after all they do have a lot of spiky characters to deal with. They have a tough job to do, in having to filter them all out. So, I can't really blame them for coming across miserable and unenthusiastic. What I can't forgive is them tarring everyone with the same brush, which is exactly what most of them do. They see a young person and make an immediate assumption that you're trying to cheat the system and you're not putting any effort into your job searches whatsoever.

This annoys me because as well as all the types of people I've described to you, there are also many genuine ones who are trying their best to get a job. They don't deserve to be talked down too, like they're the scum of the earth!

What I used to hate most of all was the inconsistency of it all. One week I had to face a painstakingly lengthy interrogation, and however much evidence I produced, it was never enough to satisfy them. They always managed to find fault with something. The next time, I went even more prepared. I took a bag full of evidence showing all my job applications and confirmations going back several months. This time I see a younger adviser who doesn't ask me a single job-related question. All he asks is "is it still raining out" and then sends me on my way!

It's these polar opposites that used to make going to the job centre such an unsettling experience. The fact that you could be greeted like a long-lost friend one week, and then like their worst enemy two weeks later was truly mystifying and quite frankly laughable. Also laughable was the number of jobs you were expected to apply for. A minimum of ten jobs per fortnight, if you didn't manage this, you'd risk having your benefit stopped. You may be reading this thinking, that's fair enough, people should be expected to apply for plenty of jobs, and they should be punished if they don't. The problem is, it's rare you find ten suitable jobs. So, everyone ends up applying for things they have no qualifications for and have no chance of ever getting. They do this just to avoid the wrath of the advisers.

The last time I attended the job centre I suffered a full-blown panic attack. The thought of stepping back in that building, still, even to this day, fills me with terror. It is simply not an option. In fact, I'd rather have no benefit at all than risk it. And at the time, that's exactly what I did. I lived off my savings for several months. At the time I was very confused about my health issues and didn't realise I might be entitled to a different benefit. I didn't know that employment support allowance existed. It's a big relief now, that I don't have to attend the job centre anymore. I honestly don't know how I'd cope with the pressure whilst in my current mental state, so I'm grateful for that small mercy.

MY STORY

When I went for my first medical, as well as being a nervous wreck, I was angry and disturbed by what I heard in the waiting area. It was just like being back in the job centre. People were bragging about how easy it was to play the system and plotting ways in which they could further deceive the mental health nurse. I know there are benefit cheats out there, I'm not completely naive! But I tend to see the good in people and was still shocked by what I saw. It's people like that, that make it so difficult for those of us who are truly deserving of the support. It's already hard enough having to go into detail about your illness, having to prove yourself to a total stranger, brings everything to the surface and makes you feel extremely vulnerable. I always dread having to go through another medical and know that I will be summoned again sooner rather than later. What makes it worse is that I never know the exact date and I'm constantly living on edge whilst I wait for the dreaded brown envelope to arrive!

When You're on benefits it feels like you're under constant scrutiny, like everything you do has a hidden agenda, and you must justify your every move. When your illness genuinely prevents you from working, the only opinion that truly counts is that of the medical professionals who have diagnosed you in the first place. However, I can't help being influenced by other people's opinions, I hate the idea of not being believed. With mental health it's much harder, as your symptoms are often only obvious to fellow sufferers. It's very difficult to explain an illness you can't see.

It's so easy to tar people on benefits with the same brush and make inaccurate assumptions. I'm ashamed to say I've done it myself. In the past, long before I had a mental health illness, I would regularly sit in the pub with the lads moaning about all those people on benefits, spending our taxpayer's money, whilst living a life of leisure. Television documentaries such as benefits Britain and life on the dole, don't help. Let me categorically say, we're not all like those people!

Thankfully on this occasion, with copious amounts of support from family and friends, I was able to survive the process, tick all the necessary boxes and get the benefit I was entitled too.

LET'S TALK BENEFITS!

The benefit system is confusing to say the least. Sadly, you get large quantities of genuine cases still slipping through the net, people who are clearly not fit to work but somehow still fail their medicals. Today I'm going to look at some of the reasons for this, and the flip side, where people get what they don't deserve, simply because they know how to work the system. I'm also going to share what it's like having to live with a long-term health illness, having to rely on benefits and how you're perceived by others, whilst you're doing this. How much of this is a fair judgement and how much is completely unreasonable.

THE DREADED MEDICAL

There can be numerous reasons why genuinely ill people fail their medicals. Obviously nerves on the day can have a huge influence, you're already in a highly sensitive state, and having to rely on one person deciding your fate like this, is extremely daunting to say the least. I know lots of people who have life altering disabilities and most of them are incredibly positive in nature, as they try their best to get on with things, despite their circumstances. They refuse to moan about their limitations or any discomfort they may be feeling. My dad was one of these people.

The whole process starts with a lengthy form to fill in, with hundreds of tedious questions, most of which are completely irrelevant to you and your condition! It's hardly surprising to us, that my dad didn't lay it on thick enough with his answers, and his claim was declined. We encouraged him to appeal the decision, as did his doctor. In 2010, my dad passed away. A few days after his death he received a letter saying that his appeal had failed and in their expert opinion he was fit for work. I won't go into detail about his condition or how the family reacted to this letter, but needless to say, he was far from fit for work, and we were angry and bemused by the decision.

My dad is one of many cases just like this, not to mention those who have committed suicide, shortly after their benefits have been stopped or they have had a sanction issued. It's a hard thing to prove either way, so I don't have any accurate statistics on this. However, I have read some alarming stories online from families of deceased, who are convinced that a benefit decision has led to their loved ones taking their life. A friend of mine works at a local food bank and she tells me that the number of people coming in, who have been sanctioned by the job centre, is getting out of hand. She describes these people as being in a desperate state, feeling completely degraded and often in floods of tears by the time they arrive.

Imagine a non-swimmer being made to swim across a lake in order to get their allowance. They want to do it, they desperately need to do it, but it's just not possible. I live in fear of being put on a lower rate of benefit, not because of the financial implications, but due to the unrealistic requirements I'd have to meet. Sometime, In the not-too-distant future, I fear this will happen. I'll have to attend job groups which are held in the town centre. My illness prevents me from getting into populated areas like this, let alone into a busy, unfamiliar environment. It's hard for people to understand unless they also suffer with severe anxiety, you could literally offer me a million pounds and I still couldn't do it!

Just like the predicament facing the none-swimmer, at present this task would prove to be an impossible one. Believe me, I have tried and continue to try hard to change how I am. To not allow my anxiety to rule my life. Sadly, only myself and my family have been witness to my efforts. Frustratingly the people who make all the decisions, the people sat behind their desks, don't see all of this, and it seems they won't be happy unless I drown trying!

Lately, I keep having this recurring dream. I'm in a log cabin in the middle of nowhere with just my own thoughts for company. Whilst I stay inside, I'm perfectly safe, but outside is a pack of hungry wolves, circling the cabin, waiting for me to make my move. Eventually I start to run out of food and water, and I'm left with two options, neither of which are very appealing. Remain inside and die, or take my chances with the wolves, which will probably result in the same fate. I wake up not knowing the outcome.

All the medical professionals involved in my care have continued to advise me to take things one small, manageable step at a time. I've become adept at living in the present. When I'm asked to contemplate the future, I can't help but freeze. It's an automatic response, it's like the shutters go down, and I'm back in my protective bubble!

I'm yet to find the answer to this, but the fact is, unless you're terminally ill, you must earn to survive, and it still feels like I'm a long way off being able to do this. Meanwhile the wolves are still circling and I'm slowly but surely running out of time.

TICKING MORE BOXES!

Feeling totally inept, ashamed of what I've become and powerless to change. Every day I'm fighting against a barrage of negativity. I wish I weren't so reliant on everyone; I feel I've become an enormous drain on my family and friends. People must wonder why I can't try harder. I see the doubt in their eyes, and this saddens me. I can guess what they're thinking, that if it were them, they'd be able to fight it, they wouldn't be so weak. I've even had people say this to me. I wish they understood that depression is nothing to do with strength or weakness, I wish they could feel how I feel, just for one day.

The one person I don't feel like a burden around is my carer, the reason being obvious, she's paid to spend time with me and has no emotional attachment. That being said, I don't think she fully understands my mental health. Even though she means well, there's been an inconsistency in her approach. On meeting for the first time, she told me that we would go at my own pace, concentrate on one small task at a time and not worry if I couldn't achieve something straight away. We'd never look too far ahead and never set unmanageable goals, only ever focusing on the here and now. This was all very reassuring, and I felt positive moving forwards. However, only a few weeks in, she began to talk about meeting targets, and that her boss expected me to progress faster than I currently was. Before I knew it, she was talking about what we would have achieved four and five weeks down the line. For some reason, staying in the present had gone completely out of the window! I felt rushed and out of my depth. When I wasn't able to meet the targets she'd set, I found myself apologising profusely, as I felt I'd let her down. When I was successful at something, such as walking to the corner shop, in her eyes I'd mastered that issue, so we could tick that box and proceed to the next challenge. I really wish things where that easy for me, but that's not how living with anxiety works for anyone, and her attitude could be perceived as a bit naïve.

I have worked in mental health as a support worker and now require the services myself. This has allowed me a unique insight. One thing I know for sure, is that someone with high anxiety needs to perform a task numerous times, before they feel safe and comfortable with it. Repetition is the key. However, from a mental health workers point of view, your always under pressure to reach your targets. This of course, should never have an adverse effect on the service user, but on occasions I can see how it does. As mental health becomes more prevalent, and more people are encouraged to talk, there are many more referrals from the GP's and the individual services are becoming saturated. People like me are being passed from pillar to post. They might as well be saying *'we've done all we can for you, and now your someone else's problem!*

To put it bluntly, the system is failing. Yes, it appears like the boxes are being ticked and the services are succeeding in reaching their objectives. But what happens to the individual afterwards? Mental health doesn't just disappear overnight. Often, it's assumed that if someone fails to pick up the phone and ask for help, then they don't need it. But what if like me, your anxiety prevents you from doing this? Anxiety makes you terrified of the unknown, answering the phone can be extremely daunting. What if your too frightened to open your mail? You may end up missing appointments, which again, may come across like you don't want the support, when the reality is you desperately need it!

The threat of having my benefits taken off me, is never far from my mind. That dreaded brown envelope confirming my next medical. Just getting to the appointment is a huge feat in itself. Once there, I'm close to panic and struggle to function properly. I can't breathe let alone speak! So, my chaperone has to confirm my arrival. I can't stay in the waiting area. It's usually a tiny box room, and claustrophobic feelings will almost certainly bring on a panic attack. I wait outside for what seems like an eternity, before answering some ridiculously vague questions, in a vain attempt to prove an invisible illness. It's a nightmare, but one I must endure. It's all about playing the game and continuing to tick all the right boxes. Some find it easy, but some like my dad, tragically do not.

THE UNCOMFORTABLE TRUTH

Mental health is still an extremely uncomfortable subject to talk about, and life would be so much easier for myself and fellow sufferers if this wasn't the case.

They say that one in four of us will have a mental health illness at some stage of our lives. The reality is it's almost certainly much higher than this, but sadly most people don't seek help. Recently I was made aware of an alarming statistic that over 70% of people who commit suicide, haven't attempted to get any medical support. Often the families are left in total shock and bewilderment by the tragic event, saying that they didn't see it coming.

It fills me with sadness when I think of those people trapped in their own heads, having to deal with unimaginable mental anguish and eventually losing their battle. Feeling alone in every sense of the word, right up until the end.

Mental health is no longer a forbidden thing to talk about.

People are made aware of all the helpful organisations that exist and are being encouraged to seek help from their GPs for the first port of call. So why when the subject is at its most prevalent, do the majority, even in their darkest moments, still refuse to get help? I find the whole thing perplexing to say the least and an area that desperately needs challenging.

I grew up in a world where I was led to believe that only weak-minded people could get a mental health illness and only a negative pessimistic person would end up getting depressed. Depression not even being recognised as a proper illness, but something that people should be able to snap out of! I wonder how many still share that view today.

Mental health is not a weakness and as for depression, I for one have always been a positive upbeat person who sees the bright side of life, but I still got it! I could give you several examples of strong level-headed people who end up completely pole axed and unable to function properly, all because of this illness. Telling people that I suffer from depression is a great way to kill a conversation! Either that or they say they understand as they get a bit down sometimes too. Clearly these people don't get it and it infuriates me beyond belief. Having depression is not the same as feeling a bit down, just as having a mental health illness does not make you cuckoo or a fruitcake, or any other derogatory term I've heard used. It does not mean that you're stupid in anyway either. Look at Stephen Fry, one of the most intelligent people on the planet, but his illness has been well documented over the years.

The truth is it doesn't matter who you are, rich or poor, successful, or unsuccessful. Sure- a traumatic event might act as a trigger, but often this isn't the case. You might just be one of the unfortunate ones who happens to get it. Like any other debilitating illness, it affects people at random. No different to cancer or heart disease, mental health does not hand pick you. It has no favourites. But the facts are there, clear for everyone to see; suicide is the leading cause of death in young people aged 20-34. Just how many of these deaths could have been prevented?

I accept that society is becoming more open to talking about mental health, but there's still a terrible stigma surrounding it, which prevents individuals from seeking the help, when they need it the most. I was nearly one of those people. Terrified by the prospect of asking for help, I didn't think I was worthy of it, and worst of all, I couldn't accept that I was in any way mentally ill!

HIDDEN TRUTHS

Imagine the scene. A young adult on crutches staggers into a department store. It's clear for all to see that he's struggling and getting around the store is going to be a challenge. Most people will show empathy and kindness to him, if given the opportunity they might even offer him support. The staff are more likely to bend over backwards to help and make his shopping experience as comfortable as possible. It's possible I'm being a tad naïve in this case, but I do have experience of pushing people around shops in wheelchairs. Suddenly you find people queuing up to be helpful, opening doors, moving objects out of the way, even offering to carry your shopping for you! You're given all the time and space you need.

Getting around a department store would be extremely daunting for me and likely be even more challenging than for the person on crutches. My mental health illness is equally restrictive, but unlike the people with physical ailments, my illness goes unrecognized. On first appearance, I seem to be in perfectly good health and able to cope. In a busy environment, people are not likely to give me the space, I desperately need. My anxiety levels often make leaving the house an impossibility. Though people are becoming more educated, and perceptions are changing for the better, it's still hard for them to understand what they can't see, so sadly there is no immediate solution.

Maybe it's time we started challenging the way things have always been. If we lived in a world where we felt comfortable enough to talk openly about our mental health. In such a world, it wouldn't be unusual for someone with anxiety issues to phone up a venue, prior to their visit, to request some help. This could result in a member of staff meeting you at the front of a shop and escorting you around or even meeting you at the entrance to the train station and taking you exactly where you need to go. The possibilities are endless if you just have the confidence to ask for help in the first place. I know I have no right to preach, when I haven't even tried this myself yet, but it's certainly an option I'm going to explore in the future.

Don't be afraid to ask for help, you have as much right to it as anyone else and you might be surprised by the response you get.

What can society do?
Media and television have a huge influence over how people view mental health. But, before I get on my band wagon, It's not all bad! There's plenty of expert

phone ins on daytime television, which are informative and offer good advice and links to support groups. There are actors who portray mental health very accurately in various soaps and dramas. In Coronation street, I thought Steve McDonald's story of living with depression was a particularly good one and a few years ago Emmerdale Ashley's dementia storyline was extremely well-written. Both of which brought much needed awareness to the public. There have been several other story lines, relating to all kinds of mental health issues, from eating disorders, to bullying, loneliness, to self-harming. But just as you think the publicity is going in the right direction, on the same programs you get so many derogatory terms when referring to someone with a mental health illness.

Brain dead, Insane, Nutjob, Fruitcake, Retarded, Not all there, Nothing upstairs! Screw loose. These are just some of the terms I've heard used flippantly in the last couple of weeks, and there normally said in a humorous manner, not intended as an insult! Fair enough, I can take a joke as much as the next person, but you wouldn't expect a joke to be made about someone with cancer or a brain tumor, would you? So why accept it with mental health? and why should we be so surprised that people have trouble opening up, when this is how they're perceived?

Then you get the news stories, regularly including violent attacks by someone with a mental health illness. Of course, not everyone with mental health issues is violent, most of us know this, I hope! But what about the younger audience, what must they think?

I think the media need to include more uplifting stories relating to mental health, and I strongly believe that at school, just as much emphasis should be put on the subject, as is already put-on physical education. If we can get people talking from a young age, then hopefully perceptions will change, and more people will get the help they need.

THE HARDEST QUESTION

Through my online blog (which is no longer operational), I was asked hundreds of questions relating to anxiety and depression. Some of which, I could answer immediately due to my own experiences, and some that needed more thought. I'm not ashamed to say, I passed a few of the more technical ones on to more qualified people, sadly I don't have all the answers, but then again, I'm yet to meet anyone who does! Anyway, before I get round to sharing the most frequently asked, I'm going to start with what I find to be the hardest question of all, which is ….

Why? Seems like a simple enough question, doesn't it?

Why is it such an effort to get out of bed every day?

Why don't I want to face anyone or anything?

Why do I live in a constant state of fear?

Why do I hate myself so much?

Why did I try to kill myself again, when it seems I have so much to live for?

I'm told I'm doing well; I'm told I've come a long way, but all I see is me stuck in the mud, trudging from one failed suicide attempt to another!

In a world that's full of love for me, with the greatest most supportive family and friends you could ever wish for. I've been given so many opportunities to succeed, so why do I continue to fail? How many chances do I deserve? How long before people see me for the waste of space and huge burden I've become?

I see the utter shock in my friends faces, I see the helpless look in my brothers' eyes. I know that I'm the cause of my mothers' tears. The guilt is eating me up, its unbearable! I'm so confused, I'm so ashamed. I doubt I could feel any worse than this.

I know that depression is difficult to live with, for all concerned, not just the immediate sufferer. Families can feel helpless and start scrutinising the illness. I know they do this to try and understand it better, but most of the time the person suffering can't answer their questions and are left feeling judged. Such judgements will only make them feel abnormal and even more isolated.

Try to remember that, **Why?** May appear a simple enough question, harmless in its nature, but it Remains one of the hardest questions of all, for a sufferer of depression.

Questions & Answers:

1/ Can a depressed person be successful in life?

For people like myself who have depression, it can be hard to see any positive qualities in ourselves. That being said, **I've never met anyone without any!** The problem is getting past that relentless self-deprecating voice in your head, the one that loves nothing more than to constantly put you down and convinces you that you're useless in every way. Such a powerful and emphatic voice can be difficult to ignore, but believe me when I tell you, you're much stronger than you realise. There is no quick fix to depression, but you can learn to live with it, and despite it, by taking small manageable steps, you can go on to lead a fulfilled and successful life.

ACCEPTANCE AND APPRECIATION – First you need to accept that you have a serious life changing illness and that it's not your fault. That might sound strange, buts it's the most important stage of your journey. As I shared in the *Acceptance* chapter, it took me a long time to come to terms with my illness and stop blaming myself for it, feeling ashamed, and thinking that I was strange or weak for feeling the way I was. You can't begin to plan ways to live with depression until you have reached this stage of acceptance. Your family and friends also need to accept it, and realise that you're going to have your limitations, often plans may need to change at the last minute. If your friends don't even try to be understanding or empathetic towards you, then I would question whether they're true friends at all.

A real friend is one who walks in when the rest of the world walks out. (Walter Winchell)

When you have depression, your good days tend to be fewer and farther between. That's why it's so important to embrace these moments and make the most of whatever you love to do. I can honestly say that I appreciate the smaller things in life and take less for granted, far less than prior to me having depression.

BRAVERY- You can't tackle depression on your own. It doesn't matter how strong you think you are; you will need help. And asking for help is nothing to be ashamed of. Depression is life changing and debilitating. If you had any serious physical condition, you wouldn't hesitate. So why do so many people insist on struggling on their own, when they're suffering something that millions of people can relate too?

235

The problem is when you're battling, you're mental health, it doesn't feel this way. Instead, it seems like you're the only person in the world like this, you're painfully abnormal and nobody could possibly understand. It's a frightening, confusing time. It seems cruel to inflict your misery on others and you don't feel deserving of any support. Try to remember though, this is the depression talking. You are worthy of support and people will appreciate your honesty. It takes a lot of courage to confide in others, but it will be a huge relief when you do so. For me once I started opening up, I was surprised by just how many people could relate to my illness. I took a lot of strength from this, and it's now much easier to talk about my mental health. I no longer hide behind it.

COMPASSION AND SENSITIVITY- You need support, be it from family and friends or specific support groups, of which there are many. Most People are not going to understand your illness entirely and I wouldn't expect them to unless they've experienced its symptoms themselves. What I do expect, is for them to remain open minded and non-judgmental. If this is not the case, then these are not the kind of people you want to surround yourself with.

You need to be compassionate to yourself and recognise that this is a horrible illness to live with. In other words, cut yourself some slack, stop beating yourself up all the time and viewing every unsuccessful act as a failure. This can be a massive challenge at times, believe me I know! But at least try to give it a go.

It's not important how many setbacks we have or how many times we get knocked down. What's important is that we continue to get back up again. Finding the inner strength to battle your depression and persevere with things, despite how crap you're feeling! That is a quality which can't be underestimated. It can also be hard to find (I appreciate this), but trust me, it's in there somewhere, if you delve deep enough.

I try to think of my depression as a separate entity, or a monster if you like! The monster feeds itself on my negativity and low self-esteem, but the more I pick myself up and continue with my life, the weaker it gets, and this is hugely satisfying. I know it's not always possible, and some days it still wins the battle, but I find myself extra determined to bounce back, and I refuse to let it win the war. I realise that you may be at a different stage of your journey and I appreciate that some days it's a struggle to find any fight whatsoever. The advice I give, is that wherever possible, try not to fuel your monster.

Going back to the original question, of course you can still be successful in life, in fact, due to your struggles, you have likely developed a deeper empathy and appreciation for things. Moving forwards, you'll be more objective and less critical of others. If anything, these combined traits could make you even more successful.

2/ Is suicide a selfish act?

Most people I have spoken to are of the opinion that suicide is a selfish act. This has been the same for as long as I can remember and growing up, I shared the same view.

It doesn't help if you've been directly affected by it or know of a family who has. You've been witness to the horror and devastation left behind. It's perfectly normal at this point to mainly sympathise with the family and not give a second thought to the victim and the horrible place they must have found themselves in. What you witness is a whole world of pain and suffering, and you can't help but feel an element of resentment towards the person who caused it. It's a delicate subject, I know, but in my opinion to consider suicide as a selfish act is a huge misconception. Suicide is not a selfish act; suicide is an act of shear desperation by someone whose experiencing unimaginable amounts of inward torment. Someone who has lost all sense of hope and literally feel they have no options left.

The first time I planned to take my life, I became convinced that my family and friends would be much better off without me. I believed I was a burden to them all, and a burden on society. I longed for it all to be over, for the pain to finally stop. People's lives would be so much easier without me dragging them down.

I knew there would likely be sadness right after my death, but this didn't compare to the sadness and disruption I would cause by staying alive. When I'm so down, I don't see myself ever recovering, I'm only going to get worse and cause further distress to my family.

I guessed that my closest friends would try to take on some of the responsibility and I hated the idea of them feeling in any way to blame. I therefore wrote letters to each of them in a vain attempt to explain my actions and try to reassure them that they had been amazing friends, explaining that this was my decision alone and nothing they could have said or done would have changed the outcome. I couldn't possibly predict their emotions but I'd much rather they felt anger towards me, as opposed to guilt. These letters were extremely difficult to write. **Would a selfish person have gone to all this trouble?**

My next big concern was financial. I didn't want to leave my family with any debts. In an ideal world I would have sold my house and paid off the excess mortgage. Previously it had tenants in but at this stage the house was vacant and had been up for sale for some time. Unfortunately, I'd had no luck, the economic climate being in a poor state. However, after doing extensive research I realised that the debt of the house would die with me and my mother would not be accountable for any of it. This came as a huge relief.

I made sure I had enough money in the bank to pay for the funeral and put all my account details in a file in my top drawer. Also, in this file I put any other important information my family would need, such as my birth certificate, national insurance number, mortgage details and all the numbers they'd need to contact after my death. I was trying my best to cover all angles and make the process as simple as possible for them. **Does this sound like the actions of a selfish man?**

I didn't intend to tell anyone my plan to end my life, but as the pressure valve increased, I desperately needed some kind of release.

I chose to open up to my counsellor and in doing so I immediately felt a huge sense of relief. I didn't hold back or spare any detail, I literally told her everything.

It wasn't until a much later date when I was in a better headspace and had no intention of going through with the plan. Only then did I confide in my family and closest friends. My friends all responded in a similar manner, in complete shock. They said things like *"How could you have done that to us? How could you have possibly done that to your family?"* I couldn't blame them for asking these questions and don't get me wrong they have been amazing support to me ever since. But again, their initial reaction indicated, that they believe suicide to be a selfish act.

It's hardly surprising that people are so reluctant to talk about their mental health or admit to having suicidal thoughts. Yes, there's many organisations out there offering great support, but we can't expect the alarming statistics to go down any, unless people's attitudes drastically change.

In my opinion people need educating from a young age. Physical health is well covered at school, so why not put as much emphasis on our mental health. Everyone is likely to be affected by it at some stage of their lives, either themselves or someone they're close to. So why not get them talking about the subject as early as possible.

It needs to be accepted as a serious illness and I still have my doubts that some people do.

I've now attempted suicide on two separate occasions. The first was premeditated, planned months in advance, the second was completely spare of the moment with a more obvious trigger (I could not live with the fact that I'd lost my life savings gambling). The only similarity between the two, was that I was in an incredibly dark place with no apparent escape. Words cannot describe the inward torment I had to endure in these moments. Both were acts of sheer desperation, not selfishness!

3/ *How do I overcome my nervousness?*

For as long as I can remember I've suffered greatly with my nerves, long before I was diagnosed with an anxiety disorder. Of course, it's important that we differentiate between nervousness and anxiety. Nerves are part excitement and slight fear about certain upcoming situations. Sportsmen often say that nerves can be a good thing, and even enhance their performance. With anxiety the fears are ramped up a level, sometimes becoming irrational and often having a detrimental effect. Having an anxiety disorder is yet another level up, where your fear turns into terror and becomes uncontrollable. This can lead to panic attacks and a great deal of avoidance behaviour.

It's the fear of the unknown that leads to my anxiety, not to mention that inner self-doubting voice that we all have. Repetition and familiar routine are what work best for me. If you do something enough, it becomes second nature and you're able to switch onto auto pilot. It's fascinating to think that something as complex as the human mind, can be so easily manipulated. Meticulous planning of my day helps create the necessary illusion of being in control. It doesn't matter how accurate this is, as long as I believe it to be true, it's like a placebo effect. This can work really well when facing up to your fears, as you become comfortable and self-assured in what you're doing, you soon start to wonder what it was you were worried about in the first place!

So, providing I know what's expected of me and I have the capabilities to accomplish the task in hand, I have succeeded in overcoming my nerves, haven't I? Sadly, as you know life doesn't work like this. For me, extensive planning works to a point, in limiting the number of surprises, but it doesn't eliminate them all together. It's impossible to plan for every eventuality, and for times when you can't do this, you need some other coping strategies.

Breathing your way to success! Controlling your breathing by taking deep breathes in through your nose and out through your mouth. Focusing on your chest rhythmically rising and falling, concentrating on this alone and trying to slow everything else down to remain in that present moment.

Using positive reminders, such as a mantra that you use on a daily basis. Words such as *"I am calm and assured and in total control"* Repeating a statement like this over and over in your head, until eventually you start to believe it. Having positive messages written down and reading them before I leave the house also works for me. Some of these things may sound simple but you'll be surprised how beneficial they can be.

4/ How did you discover you were depressed and what caused it?

Such a simple sounding question, but an almost impossible one for me to answer. You could say that many accumulative factors lead to my depression or you could say that it's an Illness that picked me completely at random with no past influences or traumatic events having anything to do with it. The truth is I still don't know when or why, and that's what makes it so difficult to live with. I had a terrible time at high school dealing with being bullied on a daily basis (see High School Trauma chapter). I became extremely introverted and learnt to repress my feelings as a coping mechanism. This extended into adulthood when I continued to have no confidence and extremely low self-esteem. I kept being transported back to that little boy cowering in the corner of the school playground, as I always took on the persona of a victim (I still often do)   It took me a long time to accept that I had a mental health illness in the first place, let alone get any help for it. This can be an extremely frightening and confusing time, and perhaps you feel that by keeping quiet, it makes what your experiencing, seem less real.

For me, there was also an element of shame, what right did I have to be depressed? If I was at all! It seemed much more likely, that what I was experiencing was down to my abnormalities and not mental health related. If I couldn't understand the illness, how could I possibly expect others too. I thought I'd be harshly judged, but now I see that I was wrong about this, and I really wish I'd sought help sooner. When you do start to open up, you realise that you're not on your own after all, and that there are millions of people just like you. Millions who are trying to battle this horrible illness without any support.

Revisiting past ordeals isn't easy, but when I did begin to talk about things, I felt a huge sense of relief, like a crushing weight had been lifted from me. I was also pleasantly surprised by the response. People I least expected too, could sympathise, and relate to how I was feeling.

Several years since, whilst working in a mental health setting, I was attacked and ever since this incident I have suffered with panic attacks. I still find myself stuck in a vicious cycle of anxiety and depression, where one always effects the other. Due to my depression It's easy for me to become isolated for long periods of time. Once I do have to go somewhere or converse with someone, I now become even more anxious. As the anxiety gets the better of me, it forces me to cancel my plans, which makes me feel inadequate and even more depressed! So, in answer to your question medically speaking nothing in-particular can cause depression, however anxiety and repressed feelings can be a big contributing factor. That is why asking for help and talking therapy are so important to help you manage your illness.

5/ *What should you do if you are depressed?*

To be perfectly honest, I'm still searching for the best answer to this question. One thing for sure, is you need copious amounts of support, both from family and friends, and from medical professionals. It's very difficult to tackle this illness on your own. During your journey, you're going to receive lots of guidance, some good, some ludicrously bad! You're going to have people quite rightly, recommending regular exercise or any kind of physical activity. Keeping yourself busy and your mind occupied is also good advice. Using mindfulness to help you to live in the present and not think too far into the future is important too.

All this is great advice, and don't forget all the techniques I shared in the Coping Tools chapter. Of course, having lots of strategies to help deal with your illness is beneficial, but it can also be overwhelming, as people bombard you with yet more recommendations. Depression can be hard enough without having to deal with all this new information. You need to sift through it and pick out what works for you. Having to listen to lots of people, all of which think their methods work best, can be exhausting to say the least. Always remember they mean well, but equally, don't be afraid to tell them to back off, if it all gets too much for you. I think the best thing you can try to do is to continue to live your life. I know this is much easier said than done.

You're going to have bad days, in my experience some really bad ones! This you need to try to accept, but you also need to make the most of your good days. When you're feeling terrible, always remember that, tomorrow the suns going to rise on a brand-new day. It's important not to give up, and by living your life and embracing the moments, in effect you're putting two fingers up to your depression (figuratively speaking!)

It's not important how many setbacks we have or how many times we get knocked down. What's important is that we continue to get up. Finding the inner strength to battle your depression and persevere with things, despite how crap you're feeling! That is a quality which can't be underestimated. It's also a quality which can be very hard to find (I appreciate this), but it's in there somewhere, if you delve deep enough.

Don't Quit

When things go wrong, as they sometimes will.
When the road you're trudging seems all uphill.
When the funds are low, and the debts are high.
And you want to smile, but you have to sigh.
When care is pressing you down a bit.
Rest if you must, but don't you quit.
Success is failure turned inside out.
The silver tint of the clouds of doubt
And you never can tell how close you are.
It may be near when it seems so far.
So, stick to the fight when you're hardest hit.
It's when things go wrong that you mustn't quit.

6/ Should you mix with people who have similar mental health illnesses?

I think it's good to have a mixture of both. Of course, It's important to be around people who you can relate to and who understand better how you're feeling. People who don't have the illness can never truly empathise with you. But on the other hand, what works best for me, is surrounding myself with upbeat positive people, whereas sometimes other people suffering, may not have the most positive outlook. I used to work in a mental health setting where people came for drop-in sessions. As great and supportive a group as this was, when you get a lot of people who have depression mixing with each other, the conversation can soon get extremely dark. If one person is feeling miserable and hopeless, it's amazing how quickly this negative energy can be transferred to the entire group. You soon get people leaving the session feeling worse than when they arrived!

It's about finding the balance that works best for you. If you're having a good day, you may be better equipped to take on board someone else's problems. If you're feeling down, then doing this will only ever have a detrimental effect on your own health. Offering help and support to them can also be extremely uplifting and great for your self-worth. Suddenly you feel useful, like you have a purpose again, emotions that have been lost for a long time. Doing a good deed for someone, such as an elderly neighbour can be equally rewarding. It's a relief to become the carer for a change, instead of the one being cared for.

So, in conclusion, by all means be friends with others who have depression but be cautious and remember to look after yourself. It's a hard-enough illness to deal with, without taking everyone else's issues on board.

7/ How can I convince my girlfriend to get help for her depression?

Seeing someone you love struggling like this and refusing to get help must be extremely tough, I have never been in this position. But I am battling my own depression and accepting it took me a long time. In my opinion, pushing her into getting the help will not work, it will only result in alienating you. Yes, gently reminding her that there's lots of help out there is not a bad thing, but don't overdo it. She needs to make this decision herself. You therefore need to be patient and empathetic towards her, when possible, try to remind her what a great person she is and why you love her as much as you do. Also, when she's having a day where she's feeling less down, try to encourage her to have some fun, a gentle reminder to her that life's not all bad.

At the same time remember about your own health. There are support groups out there for you too, with likeminded people who will be able to advise you better than I can. Sometimes taking a step back might sound cruel but it can be the healthy option for both of you. Try to include more people if you can, such as friends and family.

Sometimes you may feel helpless and wish you could do more to ease your loved one's pain. Often just being there and letting them know they're not on their own, is helping more than you realise. You're not going to understand the illness entirely, no one's expecting you too, but you can still be sympathetic even though you don't fully get it, just try to remain open minded. You need to be someone your loved one can lean upon; you need to offer plenty of reassurance and at times a shoulder to cry on. But you also need to appreciate there'll be times when they want to be left on their own. Every day can be totally different, and the person suffering will experience fluctuating emotions (massive ups and downs). This can be frustrating and again hard to understand. This is when it's essential you stay patient and remain consistent with your support.

If it ever gets to a stage where you are concerned about her immediate state of mind and that she might be a danger to herself, then there are crisis numbers you can phone, you will find these on any of the big mental health websites such as Mind. I hope you don't need these, and your girlfriend accepts the help in her own time. Remember to be patient.

8/ Why do people with depression push others away?

There's lots of reasons why I push people away, the main one being unless they've had depression themselves, they can't possibly understand how I'm feeling. Even though I'm an advocate for talking about your mental health. When I'm in a depressed state everything's a huge effort and therefore having company is the last thing I want. I also don't want to inflict my negativity on to other people, I would much rather suffer in silence. Add to that, that I feel I'm a burden and don't deserve people's sympathy, and I think I've answered your question.

Of course, I tell other sufferers that it's not at all healthy to isolate yourself like this, and if you can, surround yourself with loved ones, but the truth is when I'm having one of those days and I find myself engulfed in misery, it's extremely hard to follow my own advice. This is when you need empathetic people in your corner, who don't take it to heart, when inevitably, you need some space.

9/ What can I do if I have a panic attack and completely freeze?

Having a panic attack is a terrifying experience and one that in the past I've tried to avoid at any cost. This quickly resulted in me not wanting to leave the house, feelings of inadequacy, severe confidence problems and led to a deep depression. Eventually I got to the stage where I couldn't function properly, and all these irrational fears were becoming disruptive to my life.

The experts will tell you that nobody has ever died from a panic attack. This is true but doesn't offer much comfort when you're having one! Things that can help are being with someone who understands, will offer you plenty of reassurance and will help you with exercises to calm your breathing. I would recommend you Trying to use mindfulness to return yourself to the present and focus on slowing your breathing down (I got lots of benefit from a book called Mindfulness for dummies, which showed me some simple meditation techniques).

Use of pressure points is also something I find helpful. Admittedly, not when you're in the middle of a full-blown panic attack, but if you feel one coming on or know a certain situation can trigger you're anxiety, then there are a number of points on your body that when massaged can offer some alleviation. The one I use mostly is known as the Union Valley point, found in the webbing between your thumb and index finger. If you apply a little pressure to this area and then massage it, whilst concentrating on slowing your breathing, all the time gradually loosening the pressure. This has proved to lessen my stress. This is one of many areas you can use, but I'm far from an expert, so I will leave you to do your own research on the subject. One other simple technique that works for me, is tapping the ends of my fingers with my thumb whilst counting, it can be a good distraction. You can adapt different methods to suit you. What I like is that these tried and tested techniques are simple and don't draw unnecessary attention to you.

I have benefited hugely from mindfulness, but some days still find it hard to switch off. I was advised to use a pebble for such occasions and believe it or not it really works! I place my pebble in my hand, which is smooth and cool to the touch. I immediately feel grounded and I know that this is my special time, time away from all other distractions. I often choose to carry it in my pocket when I'm away from home, and likely to feel more anxious. Holding it doesn't immediately calm me down, but it certainly helps me focus on controlling my breathing, which in turn helps prevent panic attacks. Some might say how on earth can a pebble make any difference? but it's more about what it represents. Because I associate the pebble with mindfulness and a stress-free environment, contact with it helps return me to that state of being.

Once you've been able to breathe easier, repeating a positive mantra in your head may also reassure you that you're going to be all right. Breathing into a paper bag is a tried and tested method which will stop you from hyperventilating. I believe it's something to do with getting some of the carbon dioxide back in, but don't quote me on that!

As for freezing and not being able to move, I'm afraid I can't offer a solution to that, sometimes If you're having a panic attack, you've just got to ride it out. Remember though try to avoid any obvious triggers. For example, I've had a number of attacks in busy supermarkets, so I now choose to go to the much smaller stores, if they haven't got what I want, I shop online. If possible, I always choose a quieter time to visit somewhere.

For more information on managing your anxiety see my '10 Tips on Managing Your Anxiety' chapter.

10/ What should I do if I hate my life? Is a depressed life worth living?

I'm not going to divulge too much information in order to protect her identity, but this question was posted by a teenage girl who was struggling to fit in at high school. Extremely lacking in self-confidence and believing she had nothing to offer. Sadly, she thought herself ugly, both on the inside and out. Here's my attempt at an answer to this challenging question.

I'm so sorry that you're feeling this way, it sounds like you're having a tough time at the moment. At your age I had an extremely low opinion of myself, in fact I hated most things about myself. I struggled fitting in and thought that I hated life. I was encouraged to go to the doctors who decided to get me an appointment with a child psychologist. This was the best thing for me, it really helped to have someone to unload all my bottled-up emotions on, who didn't judge me. He gave me some great advice and taught me the importance of standing tall and being proud of myself. I really think you would benefit from having someone to talk too.

You say that your ugly, but I doubt very much this is true. It's so easy to stand in front of a mirror and work your way from head to toe, highlighting all the things you're not happy with. We all do this from time to time, but what you must remember is what you see in yourself is often a totally different person than what others see in you. We all come in various shapes and sizes and we are all attracted to different qualities in each other. Its ok to be different, in fact it should be celebrated. High school can be a cruel place, where you can be penalized for your individualism. Everyone wants to be alike and follow each other around like a heard of sheep! Try to remember that this won't always be the case. As you grow up, your uniqueness will be viewed as special and intriguing. If you're being bullied this is unacceptable and you need to talk to someone about it. I understand this won't be easy and you might think it will make the situation worse, but trust me, talking will help. I saw a child psychologist once a week and he taught me how to stand up to the bullies without being confrontational and running the risk of the treatment getting worse. He was with me every step of the way and I felt much stronger with his support.

As for you feeling like you have no talent, I'm sure this isn't true either. when you're so down on yourself it's hard to see the positive. But everyone is good at something and I bet you have a lot to offer, you just don't realise your potential yet. Fair enough you don't like yourself very much at the moment, but you're only 13, you're changing all the time, your still discovering things. I'm still learning about myself and I'm 40!

In conclusion, please don't give up on yourself and please ask for help.

11/ *How do you recover from big failure and embarrassment? My last presentation flopped and I'm freaking out about the next one!*

As well as celebrating your achievements in life, you need to also accept that you'll have to deal with disappointments. If you allow yourself to learn from the experience you can actually use it as a positive thing moving forward. Don't view it as a failure, view it more as a learning curve. It's true, we learn so much more from our mistakes than we do from our successes.

Thomas Edison wrote *'We haven't failed. We now know a thousand things that won't work, so we're that much closer to finding what will.'*

Try not to give yourself such a hard time, you're only human after all and we've all been in that situation, where things have not gone to plan, and we feel painfully embarrassed in front of a group of piers. As hard as it might sound right now, not taking things so seriously and learning to laugh at yourself is a great attribute to have. I know this is not easy to do but try putting the incident into perspective, nobody died, it's not the end of the world! you'll have more opportunities in the future to put it right.

In the build up to an important presentation it's perfectly natural to suffer from nerves and there's lots of techniques you can use to try and manage your anxiety levels. In this book I share some of the methods which have worked best for me. Look at ten tips on managing your anxiety, or if you want to read how I deal with my own anxiety (or sometimes don't!), try my social anxiety chapter. It may help you realise that we're all challenged by our daily anxieties and you're not in any way abnormal for feeling the way you do.

12/ Why are some people blessed to have blissfully happy lives, whilst others live in pain and unhappiness?

I regularly feel this way and have asked this very same question. Due to my mental health problems, I often see the world in a less than positive light! One of the most common theological questions is, if there is a god, why does he allow so much suffering? Why does he let people be born into poverty? It hardly seems fair that some people are at such a disadvantage right from the start of their lives. Sadly, I don't possess the answer to this. However, I do believe we're here to learn, and we're all dealt a certain hand, we need to try to make the most of what we've got and appreciate what opportunities arise for us. It's all a learning curve. Yes, there are people who appear to be blessed with blissful lives, but probably not as many as you think and there's likely to be plenty much worse off than you. Life's not easy and most people really struggle at stages of it. Sometimes, looks can be deceiving, someone could be very wealthy. On the surface they appear to have all that they need, but they may lack a loving family to share it all with. I know which I'd rather have. On bad days I have to cope with much inner pain, that's hard for people to understand unless they have depression themselves. On days like this I wish they could feel how I feel, but I'd like to believe this makes me appreciate the good days more than most. You just have to accept your limitations (we all have them!) and make the best of what you've got.

I find it intriguing that right now, somewhere in the world, somebody is experiencing delight, feeling truly blessed and basking in the sunshine of life- whilst someone else is experiencing total despair, a heavy affliction, a nightmare they feel will never end. It hardly seems fair, does it? But the interesting thing is that at some stage, most of us will experience the extremities of both these powerful emotions. I have lived through extreme mental pain and suffering (having clinical depression isn't much fun!). When I reached my limit of despair, I attempted to take my life. At this point, if somebody had told me I'd ever feel happiness again, I wouldn't have believed them, in fact I'd have probably punched them in the face! I couldn't imagine ever smiling again, let alone laughing and having fun with family and friends. But life goes on, I have laughed, and I have cried. I will continue to have good days and continue to have bad ones. This is the same for most people, irrespective of their mental health.

There will be times when you're having a bad time of it, it's an inevitable part of life. Bad luck can sometimes seem infectious, especially when we're in a highly sensitive state, it's so easy to blow things out of proportion and start to believe that you're the most cursed person on the planet! It may sound harsh, but the chances are this isn't true, and you're allowing self-pity to get the better of you. If you search deep enough you will find some positives and learn to relish all the good moments. I guess what I'm trying to say, is we need to play the game, take the rough with the smooth and most importantly try to enjoy the ride!

13/ *Do people ever truly recover from depression?*

Let me start by saying, you can have depression but still live a fulfilled life. I know people who have almost got the better of it, but I'm not sure they ever truly overcome it. I'm sure they'll be people who disagree with me on this, but I have depression and I believe I'll be battling the illness for the rest of my life. On my bad days, I still struggle to lift my head from the pillow and face the world. The difference is, a few years ago, one painful day of misery used to blend into the next, whereas now, I'm able to make the most of it, when the depression loosens its grip and even allow myself to enjoy aspects of life again. I guess what I'm trying to say, is that even when I'm struggling, I now realize I won't be feeling this way indefinitely, and hopefully over time the good days will start to outnumber the bad ones. This might all sound a little negative but believe me when I say, I'm much more optimistic than I used to be. One thing I don't want to do is give false hope.

Medical professionals talk about supporting you to recovery. I hate this word. With a lot of great support, I have learnt to manage my depression, but I'm far from recovered from it. Does this mean that I've failed? Does it mean I'm not a strong enough person? Of course, it doesn't! Overuse of the word recovery can put unnecessary pressure on people and leave them feeling extremely bad about themselves and even more anxious about the future. Depression is not a quick fix; You'd think the word recovery would offer you some hope, but in my experience, it can have the opposite effect. When it was used in my care, it made me feel hopeless, because I didn't believe it possible to get to the stage, they wanted me to get too. Truthfully, I still don't. I found myself asking myself the question what if I never recover? What if I have depression for the rest of my life? Is that even an option? The more the so-called experts banged on about recovery, the more I believed living with depression was not an option, and if I couldn't fix myself, I'd have no further options left to me-other than suicide. I now realise this is far from the truth. I continue to discover ways to live with my depression and enjoy aspects of life, despite of my illness. One of the main reasons I now write about it, is to share some of these methods with fellow sufferers. Too many people see things in black and white, you have depression- you get the help you need- then you recover! This is when having a bit of perspective and realising it's not as simple as that, really helps. Sure, it's important to keep optimistic about the future but you also need to be realistic and allow for what is a serious illness. Remember too that no one can predict the future, the only thing you can be remotely in control of is the here and now.

14/ Do you have faith in humanity?

Yes, very much so. I may be naive in saying so, but I strongly believe there's more good in this world than bad, it just goes unreported. Our human nature is to help people, and this is often most evident when a tragedy occurs, as the whole community pulls together to help those in need. This is happening right now, as we collectively deal with the corona virus pandemic.

Both my mother and I have difficulty getting out of the house at times, myself, due to my anxiety and my mother due to her mobility issues. Our neighbours and friends have been incredibly supportive during this time, offering to do our shopping for us, getting us whatever essentials we need, but more than that, they have taken time to phone us to check in from time to time. We have been looked after, both in a practical and emotional sense. Most of us have it in us to do the right thing by others and treat people as we'd hope to be treated ourselves. If you were following someone on the street and they unknowingly dropped a ten-pound note, I'm guessing you would pick it up, catch them up and give it back, I honestly think that 9 out of ten of us, or probably even more than that, would do the same. We can't start letting the 1 in 10 people of the world influence how we feel about the whole of humanity.

Incredible acts of kindness and generosity take place every day were people go above and beyond to help others, sadly these things don't always make the 6-o clock news but please remember they are happening at a much higher rate than all the atrocities, they just don't get people's attention in the same way. Earlier in my book I wrote about my inspirations, remarkable people who achieve great things, often against all the odds. These are the positive stories I choose to focus on, rather than becoming disillusioned by the everyday news headlines.

One positive story that did make the news was back in 2017 when a family got into difficulty at a beach in Florida. They were swimming in the ocean and inadvertently became too far from the beach. They got trapped in a strong riptide and didn't have the strength to swim out of it. They were being swept further out to sea and the more they fought against it, the more exhausted they became. Obvious panic set in, as they were now fighting for their lives! Some people on the beach saw the commotion and recognised they had to act fast to avoid a tragedy. Over 80 people joined hands to form a human chain which was able to extend far enough to rescue the family. It's a remarkable story that I'd recommend you looking up. All those people willingly put themselves at risk, in order to save, what were complete strangers to them. If this doesn't instil your faith in humanity, I don't know what will!

15/ How do you do you deal with depression without help from friends or medication?

Even though there are things you can do to manage the illness, it's extremely difficult to go through on your own. If you don't have a support network of friends and family, there are other options open to you, in fact you'll be surprised by what's out there. Your first port of call should always be your doctor. I know it's a daunting step, but it's one you desperately need to take if you haven't already. They will be patient and empathetic with you and help you get the required support. Talking therapy worked well for me. I saw a counselor for 18 months, just having someone to confide in, in an environment where I felt completely safe, was a huge relief. Together we came up with coping strategies that I still use to this day. This didn't happen overnight, it involved gaining trust over a long period of time. The important thing to remember, is that these people are professionals and just like your doctor, they understand that depression isn't a quick fix! They will not rush you.

My doctor also referred me to a mental health support group. I had a community nurse come out to assess my needs. This was all done in the comfort of my own home. I had been diagnosed with an anxiety disorder as well as the depression and so my care package was centered around this. I didn't think they would be able to help me, as I wouldn't be able to attend any of the groups, I was finding it hard enough just leaving the house! Instead of this I was designated a support worker to come out to me. I was introduced to them gradually and when I felt comfortable with him, even then, everything was done at my own pace.

We did something called graded exposure work which over a long period of time encouraged me to take small steps to doing more things on my own, things which at the time seemed like impossible tasks.

You may need one to one support, like I did, or you may benefit from group therapy with people who can relate to your illness. There are many fantastic support groups out there and your doctor will advise you on the ones available in your area. If you prefer, or don't have the confidence to attend, such groups can also be found online. I appreciate it's an effort to interact with people when you have depression, but try your best not to become isolated, it's not an illness I'd advise battling on your own.

As for the medication, there are many helpful techniques you can use on your own, such as mindfulness meditation, use of pressure points, positive messages, and mantras. All of which I have shared earlier in the book. These are all useful aids, but should be used alongside the medication, not instead of it. I understand your apprehensions when it comes to relying on medication, in the past I refused to take any tablets, even paracetamol to overcome a headache. I always believed I could overcome ailments or illnesses naturally. I quickly realised this wasn't the case when it comes to depression. I know

Antidepressants can get a bad press, but once you're on the best type for you, at the correct dosage (your doctor will help you discover this), you will feel the benefit. Taking my medication has just become a way of life, a small part of my daily routine, such as brushing my teeth. It's no big deal, and now that I'm settled, I no longer suffer with any side effects.

16/ How can depression be our teacher?

This question, unlike the others, is not frequently asked. However, I think it's both interesting and relevant, so I've chosen to include it.

I'm not sure I could ever describe depression as my teacher. when It takes its grip over me, life is extremely difficult, and I have to endure much inward torment. Simple tasks such as getting washed and dressed in a morning, suddenly become a huge challenge. Because of this, it's hard to view depression as anything but my enemy. However, and I'm now in danger of contradicting myself! I believe I'm a better person from battling the illness, and especially from being a suicide survivor. I have learnt to take much less for granted and on the rare occasions I'm having a good day, I appreciate more about life. whatever it is, be it a beautiful sunrise, a soak in a hot bath or a chocolate treat from the bakery! All the simple pleasures that in the past have passed me by, are now highlighted and take on a much bigger significance. I'd like to think I've become a more rounded person, who can show a deeper sensitivity and understanding. I don't always view things on face value, as I previously may have. Due to my plight, and this newfound open mindedness, I am a great deal more empathetic towards others.

17/ Please help me, I've lost all hope, I can't take the sadness anymore. I'm starting to think that suicide is the only option left for me. What can I do?

Dear Friend,

I'm not going to insult your intelligence by saying that I understand exactly what you're going through, nobody can. I can only imagine the pain and anguish you must be in to have reached this point. I don't know you, so I won't patronise you by saying I've been in the same place. That being said, I have been in an extremely dark place. I have felt sheer pain and desperation. I have believed that I was completely out of options and that there was no other way out. Does this sound familiar?

I came very close to the edge, but in the end choose life over death, **I want you to do the same.**

I WANT YOU TO LIVE but much more importantly **I WANT YOU TO WANT TO LIVE.**

However bad things seem, there's always hope. Even though you may not see it right now, please don't give up.

Never fear shadows. They simply mean that there's a light somewhere nearby.

Even a small star shines in the darkness.

I am grateful to you for taking the time to read this, and the fact that you continue to read it, shows me that a small part of you, however tiny, is still wanting to reach out, and for that **I am so proud of you.**

You may feel like a burden, like your family and friends would be better off without you here, I **PROMISE YOU THIS IS NOT TRUE.**

The chances are, they would be astonished if they knew you felt this way.

Remember you are not alone, you are special, and your life matters to me. You have much more to offer than you realise. You are as important as anyone else, your life is so precious.

Maybe it's time to close this chapter of your life and open a new one. I won't pretend it's going to be easy. It might even feel impossible at first, but please be patient with yourself and try to keep things simple.

Don't look to far ahead, we can only control the here and now.

Every great journey begins with a single step, and you've took that first step today. You are brave and courageous for even reading this far.

You might not be ready to talk, let alone ask for help, but when you are, remember you're a good person and you deserve the best.

Sharing my feelings and unloading my bottled-up emotions was a great relief. It felt like a huge weight had been lifted and I could breathe again. I'm not saying it will be the same for you, but if you've reached rock bottom, **<u>what have you possibly got to lose?</u>** Now, the only way is up. You might feel alone, but you're not. The reality is you are part of the biggest club in the world. There are so many people that can relate, people who may too be suffering in silence. It can feel exhausting to talk at first, but trust me, it will help, and it will get easier to do so. Seeing people at different stages of their journeys will also help, as it gives you hope that progression is possible. Below is a list of numbers and websites that may be of help to you. Once you're able to confide in your doctor, which I urge you to do, they will direct you to the appropriate support in your locality.

MIND - WWW.mind.org.uk 0300 123 3393

BEFRIENDERS – www.befrienders.org

C.A.L.M (campaign against living miserably)- 0800 585858

C.A.L.L (community advice and listening line)- 0800 132737

TIME TO CHANGE – www.time-to-change.org.uk

SAMARITANS – www.samaritans.org free call 116 123

SANE – www.sane.org.uk 0300 304 7000

RETHINK – www.rethink.org 0300 5000 927

SHOUT – www.giveusashout.org/

CHILDLINE – 0800 1111 www.childline.org.uk

NHS 111 – either view the website or dial 111

CARERS UK – www.carersuk.org>talk-to-us

ACKNOWLEDGEMENTS

I'd like to start by thanking Jake for his brilliant illustrations on the front cover.

A quick shout out to Heather who helped me with the editing.

My mother and brother for their continued loving support and patience.

My best friends Tom and Simon who both go above and beyond to make sure I'm alright and drop everything at a moment's notice if I'm not.

All my friends and teammates from my table tennis life. My hobby is an amazing escape for me, but it wouldn't be manageable without so many understanding people.

Mick and Phil who I refer to as my two adopted dads, who take me for walks and games of snooker. They are never far away when I need them.

My ex-counsellor Nicky who got me talking and accepting of my mental health. She also encouraged me to get the help I desperately needed.

All the professionals who have been involved in my care over the years, including my doctor who always has my back.

Printed in Great Britain
by Amazon

64374417R00159